ONE-CLICK TO GIVE

Jeremy Berman & Nick Black

ONE-CLICK
TO GIVE

Future Proof Your
FUNDRAISING
with Social Media

 | Books

Published by Advantage Books, Charleston, South Carolina.
An imprint of Advantage Media.

ADVANTAGE is a registered trademark, and the Advantage colophon is a trademark of Advantage Media Group, Inc.

Printed in the United States of America.

10 9 8 7 6 5 4 3 2 1

ISBN: 978-1-64225-671-0 (Hardcover)
ISBN: 978-1-64225-670-3 (eBook)

Library of Congress Control Number: 2023915219

Cover design by Megan Elger.
Layout design by David Taylor.

This publication is designed to provide accurate and authoritative information in regard to the subject matter covered. It is sold with the understanding that the publisher is not engaged in rendering legal, accounting, or other professional services. If legal advice or other expert assistance is required, the services of a competent professional person should be sought.

Advantage Books is an imprint of Advantage Media Group. Advantage Media helps busy entrepreneurs, CEOs, and leaders write and publish a book to grow their business and become the authority in their field. Advantage authors comprise an exclusive community of industry professionals, idea-makers, and thought leaders. For more information go to **advantagemedia.com**.

To Laura and Amanda,

For always having our backs and supporting our journey. It's because of you that we can do what we love. And for that we're forever grateful.

To the nonprofits we're privileged to serve,

Your tireless efforts to effect change are what keep us motivated each and every day. We won't stop until you can give a personal experience to every supporter.

CONTENTS

INTRODUCTION

The Giving Dilemma

Meet your authors: Jeremy Berman and Nick Black, tech and philanthropy entrepreneurs. As cofounders of GoodUnited, they are experts in understanding why and how donors give to their favorite causes. They've worked with nonprofits across the country to help them maximize their fundraising potential and to establish a one-on-one relationship with each supporter of their cause.

Jeremy: How long have we been on this fundraising journey, Nick?

Nick: It's been a while, man. At this point, we've been partnering with and supporting nonprofits in their fundraising for probably over a decade? Hard to imagine that.

Jeremy: It's true. At this point, it's like we've seen every single kind of fundraiser you could possibly imagine. Some of the stories you've told me from your time fundraising for Stop Soldier Suicide makes me think about all the wild ways people have tried to get the funds to keep their organizations running. The poker night for example?

Nick: Now, the poker night we had to put a stop to—couldn't encourage gambling. But then we had the rodeo clowns, the brewery tours, the motorcycle rides, and, I mean, who could forget the wine night?

Jeremy: Right, I remember that one! That turned out to be a—

Nick: A nightmare, man. Fundraising really feels like an exercise in futility sometimes. You have to pull together a team, then you gotta plan the event, then you must market the event to make sure people come, and, after all that work, you have to host the event itself. I mean, it's just a herculean task and at the end of it, you sometimes feel like you haven't gotten anywhere.

> **Thousands of people contributing $5, $10, $20 compound into high gains for a fundraising campaign.**

Jeremy: That can be disheartening for the fundraising team at a nonprofit. Like you're putting in all this effort just to get the bare minimum to keep your operations afloat.

Nick: Sure, and these extravagant fundraising events often inspire wealthy donors to give year after year—ensuring they have the budget to do their work. In our time working with nonprofits, we've found that these big gala events help those wealthy donors feel connected to the impact of their donation.

Jeremy: But wealthy people aren't the only kind of donors that give to a nonprofit's cause. This is becoming even more apparent as fundraising has become more decentralized with companies like GoFundMe or Facebook getting involved. Thousands of people contributing $5, $10, $20 compound into high gains for a fundraising campaign.

These accumulated microdonations have become a huge source of revenue for nonprofits. Yet many nonprofits continue to operate like social giving is just a flash in the pan and focus their efforts on their high-ticket donors.

So, why shouldn't the person who gave five dollars get that same connection? This question became a huge driver for the work that we do at GoodUnited today. It wasn't always easy. We had some success, but that only came from the lessons we learned through our failures.

Nick: Our many, many failures.

Jeremy: [laughs] And that's why we wanted to write this book! To share our experiences in the nonprofit arena to help nonprofits maximize their fundraising potential in a way that feels authentic to their organizational mission. I think we both know how hard it is to keep a nonprofit running. Every year it can feel like more and more resources are needed to accomplish just the basics. As time goes on, a nonprofit's fundraising department grows larger just to keep up with the demands of the operations. These two things—fundraising and operations—can sometimes feel at odds with each other. This became clear to me when I first started volunteering with nonprofits.

It was 2008, and I was working at a consulting firm when the financial crisis hit. At that time, instead of laying people off, my company decided to allow employees to take a sabbatical of up to three months to do volunteer work. During that time, we would still receive a portion of our salary and maintain all our benefits. This gave me the opportunity to step back and to explore something that I felt passionate about. When I heard about it, I immediately volunteered—it seemed like something I had to do.

I decided that I wanted to find an international volunteer experience where I could enrich the lives of kids through sports. You see,

I had already been doing this through various other organizations stateside. In my search, I found this one surf school in South Africa that worked with a local group called Penny's Way. This school used surfing lessons to reinforce good behavior in kids that were experiencing poverty the likes of which I hadn't seen before.

Penny of Penny's Way is an absolute saint of a woman. She started the school with a big dream and very little money. The school building was incredibly basic—two rooms, no running water, and very few toys and supplies. When we weren't surfing, we taught two- to five-year-old children basic reading and writing skills. And when we were on the water, we taught hang tens and cutbacks while mentoring these young minds.

Before long, however, my responsibilities at Penny's Way changed. The school was running out of cash to keep them open. Surfing and teaching became D-list priorities, and fundraising became my major concern. So, I switched out the surf suit for my consulting polo and began to work on a fundraising plan. We spent weeks organizing locals, planning strategies, and making connections with local philanthropists. We spoke to politicians, or anyone within our limited network that could connect us with someone with the means to donate. We even went door to door to try and solicit donations. And yet, we were wildly unsuccessful.

Fundraising with Penny's Way was definitely challenging, but despite our failures, I had never felt more passionate or inspired by the work I was doing. When I returned to the United States, I began to prepare for a career change. I knew I wanted to combine my consulting skills and my IT background to help nonprofits fundraise more effectively. At the same time, I had this huge entrepreneurial drive that kept me involved in the startup community. I knew working at an individual nonprofit wasn't the right course for me. With all of this in mind, I applied to business school at the University of North Carolina. That's where I met Nick.

Nick: Yeah, but not until after we graduated. We chatted about my experiences with *Stop Soldier Suicide*, the nonprofit I founded to provide mental health support to returning service members. I remember commiserating with you about how tough it is for a nonprofit to fundraise and keep operations going. Money is the complicated part of a nonprofit. But we *do* all need it to pay the bills so that we can accomplish our missions. I didn't start Stop Soldier Suicide to get rich—I started it because I wanted to save the lives of returning soldiers who were dealing with real trauma.

When I returned from deployment in 2011, out of my whole battalion of 120, we hadn't lost a single soldier. A huge achievement. I know everyone was looking forward to being back home after a long deployment. But, as I was adapting to life back, one of my fellow service members took their own life. I was shocked, as were the others in my battalion. How could you survive the war that we all served in together, come home, and then decide to end it?

That's when I knew that I had to do something to help those who served and were returning with real mental health problems—not just with us, but everywhere. To do that, I needed people and resources. I had to set up a helpline that soldiers could call for help. To keep those helplines on twenty-four hours a day, seven days a week, I needed employees with various certifications to deal with the sensitive nature of these calls. To get all that up and running, I needed cash. And this started the odyssey of suffering that I call fundraising.

Jeremy: I remember you complaining about fundraising one night that we had you and your wife over for dinner. It reminded me of the impact I felt I had when I was working with the kids at Penny's Way and how I lost track of that when I started fundraising.

Nick: I think this is when we first landed on that problem statement that we found GoodUnited on. How do we connect people to the impact of their donation? How can a nonprofit create a community around its cause?

Jeremy: The idea that a nonprofit can have a deep one-on-one relationship with each of their donors was very appealing to us. I knew there was a way we could use emerging technology to create those connections that could be so valuable for nonprofits. Yet it took us many ideas and iterations to finally figure out what would work.

Nick: Yeah, everything from an automated newsletter with the latest news on fundraising to a fundraising solution that was more gift registry than dollars donated. We really did try it all, and, after a lot of failures, there were times we felt like just folding.

> How do we connect people to the impact of their donation? How can a nonprofit create a community around its cause?

Jeremy: But we couldn't give up. We could either die by a thousand paper cuts, or we could try something new and bold.

Nick: So, we buckled down and really interrogated our mission. Failure was such a core element to what we were doing at the beginning of GoodUnited that it shifted our approach from a "we need to succeed now" mindset to one based in "fail often and fail fast." That mindset is still with us today. Now, our teams iterate around a problem, test out a solution, and scrap it if it doesn't meet our mission.

Jeremy: From those failures, we learned a lot. Even in our successes, we learned too! Through it all, we've taken that experience into our partnerships with nonprofits from across the country. Through the power of social giving, we show them how they can have a one-on-one relationship with each of their donors. Together, our nonprofit partners have collectively raised over $1 billion through social channels since partnering with GoodUnited. All through a frictionless, one-click to give experience that makes giving easy for their donors. What's more, our partners have energized their communities of fundraisers and donors that make their mission possible.

Now, we're ready to share how we did all that with you. In the following chapters, we'll show you how social giving, a new mode of fundraising, has been making digital-first fundraising the new normal. By engaging your social media channels and investing in your digital strategy, you'll create a strong and sustainable community around your cause that will create new revenue streams for your organization.

Nick: While we've talked a lot about how grueling fundraising can be, the folks doing this work should take a moment to remind themselves of why they're doing this work. It can be easy to forget about your organization's cause while raising enough funds to keep the lights on. To them I say, remember why you started your nonprofit. Bring that reason into your fundraising. Envision it as a necessary part of accomplishing your organization's mission. Doing good is definitely not easy, and making a real impact means you might crash a few times on your journey.

Jeremy: Yep, but when you invite your donors along for the ride, you've got people who can navigate your nonprofit to its ultimate destination.

CHAPTER ONE

A New Wave in Fundraising

Nonprofits represent the best of us. The people who run them tirelessly give the most of themselves to accomplish a near-impossible mission. Those who seek careers in the nonprofit world often sacrifice high salaries from corporate jobs in order to impact a cause they care about. And the causes nonprofits handle are in no way easy to accomplish. These organizations take on huge missions in the hope that they might change the world for the better. Curing cancer, ending hunger, saving whole populations of animals, ensuring human rights for marginalized communities—these and many more are the goals of some nonprofits. With such lofty missions, however, they often have a miniscule budget directed toward their operations. Nevertheless, they continue their work because they believe in their cause.

But nonprofits can't run on goodwill alone. To close the gaps in their budget and continue their activism, they must fundraise, and they must do it often. And they don't just do it in one way. From fundraising mailers to in-person events, nonprofits employ various tactics in their fundraising campaigns to continue their operations. As time goes on, a nonprofit's fundraising department may grow larger just to keep up with the demands of operations. This puts an immense amount of pressure on the fundraising team. Their success or failure doesn't just mean lost revenue for nonprofits. It could mean lost meals for hungry kids, lost time in the lab to research a deadly disease, and even lost lives of those who couldn't get the support they needed in time.

If you've been in the nonprofit sector for a while, you've seen how fundraising has drastically changed over the past few decades. The history of giving is a long one that has gone through many waves of donor behavior. The first way donors used to give was through mailed checks sent via direct mail. Then, the emergence of the internet led to online donation pages that were followed up with email blasts. These tactics, while still useful today, represent the donor behavior of yesterday. As newer generations access wealth, they are more comfortable with donating on the channels where they're spending their time—like social media. Many nonprofits, however, continue to fundraise like it's 1998 for fear that more innovative methods of fundraising are too risky. And who can blame them? Their margins for success are razor thin, and they know what works for them and their donor base.

Yet, in the past few years, a new kind of giving has been putting checks into the mailbox of nonprofits across the country. In 2017, Facebook first launched its fundraising capability for nonprofits, which started a revolution in fundraising known as social giving. *Social giving* is fundraising powered by social connections. You may be familiar with this term as it relates to peer-to-peer and crowd-funding campaigns on platforms like GoFundMe. The "social" aspect of social giving, however, more commonly refers to the connections between people that exist on social media networks such as Facebook, Instagram, and TikTok. This new mode of fundraising creates a frictionless donor experience, expands awareness into new donor groups, and represents a force multiplier for your fundraising efforts.

There is a shift in donor behavior happening right now, and it is inspired by the power of social giving. Today, there are donors who prefer to give virtually by clicking on a "donate" button they might see on Facebook under a friend's birthday. And in that one click, they can give instantly. This makes the transaction simple and frictionless. No need to pull out your checkbook. The ubiquity of social media also means they can give wherever they want and whenever they want, transforming one-day fundraising "marathons" into a twenty-four-seven giving experience. In truth, many large-ticket fundraising events like 5ks and walkathons cost more to run today and result in fewer overall donations. While part of this is the ease provided by social giving, the COVID-19 pandemic pushed all of us toward digital experiences.

During stay-at-home orders, consumer behavior changed and it impacted every industry including nonprofits. Over grabbing a table at a restaurant, we ordered takeout. Online shopping skyrocketed while large storefront retailers like J.Crew and Neiman Marcus went bankrupt. Movies were premiering on streaming services instead of in theaters. While we were all getting used to this convenience, nonprofit fundraising teams were panicking. A downtrodden economy and depressed job market meant many donors had less to give than they would have had previously. In addition, those big in-person events that accounted for a large part of their fundraising budget became too risky to host for fear of spreading the virus. What little supporters did have available to donate was often directed to pandemic-related causes (and rightfully so during those early and uncertain months).

As a result, the nonprofit sector had to get creative. While fundraising departments sought the support of donor-advised funds and planned gifts, they still struggled to make ends meet, even when foundations lessened the red tape separating organizations from much-needed grant funding. Many nonprofits turned to their communities on social media in order to raise what they needed. In many ways, GoodUnited was key in helping nonprofits pivot fundraising efforts to social. At GoodUnited, we were already partnering with nonprofits from various causes who seek to turn their social media following into real support. In doing this work, we discovered that social giving supercharged the fundraising potential of our partner organizations. Social giving, along with our expertise, helped our partners exceed their revenue goals and reach new categories of untapped donors.

In today's postpandemic world, this donor behavior has changed little: they still want to donate easily, on their own terms, and on the social media platforms where they are spending their time. While social giving won't replace legacy fundraising tactics that have supported your nonprofit thus far, it represents a new, additive, method of fundraising that allows you to develop deep relationships with each member of your donor base. Through social giving, nonprofits are able to create fundraising campaigns that appeal to the most niche interests of their donor base.

One example of this is Challenges on Facebook, a time-bound, virtual fundraising experience entirely within the Facebook ecosystem. Everything from registration (Facebook Ads) to building community (Facebook Groups) to fundraising (Facebook fundraising) to activity logging and coaching (Messenger) is all in Facebook, creating a frictionless experience every step of the way. We'll go into more detail on these later, but these Challenges were malleable enough that they can appeal to almost any kind of donor. Nonprofits who traditionally held marathons and 5ks experimented with book reading and knitting challenges to capture donors who have interests other than physical activity. With its adaptability and ease of use, social giving allows you to tailor your fundraisers to the needs and passions of your donors.

Since our founding, GoodUnited's mission has been to help nonprofits everywhere develop a one-on-one relationship with every member of their donor base. As we mentioned earlier, we've counseled nonprofits across the country on their social giving strategies and how they can deploy them to maximize their fundraising potential. For Project Purple, a nonprofit dedicated to fighting pancreatic cancer, social giving helped them reach their base when they most needed it. Their use of social media also strengthened their relationship with existing Project Purple donors and created a community of new donors who now support their mission.

Project Purple

At the start of the pandemic, Project Purple made some big bets to maximize their fundraising. While the deadly COVID-19 virus raged across the globe, pancreatic cancer still claimed lives, causing heartbreak for families across the country. In order to continue this fight during a global health emergency and at a time of economic upheaval, Project Purple redirected nearly all of their resources to raise funds for a world without pancreatic cancer. They hosted forty-seven virtual fundraising events to engage their donor base in the only place they knew was safe for people to gather—the internet. They also encouraged their strongest supporters to set up Facebook birthday fundraisers to help raise the funds they needed. Despite their efforts, however, they found the odds were against them: their campaigns resulted in confusing data and no real impact on their overall fundraising. Times were dire, and they needed a lifeline to continue the fight against pancreatic cancer.

In the past, Project Purple's team relied on their strong network of supporters from their legacy fundraising events. In this shift to digital, however, they were struggling to connect with their base through social channels. That's when they came to GoodUnited to make sense out of their social giving strategy. While their team knew the value of social giving, they didn't know how to turn their work on Facebook into actionable information, real connections with supporters, and an overall increase to their fundraising potential. They were receiving some donations from Facebook, but the platform provided no donor information. This prevented the team from following up to thank their donors for their support. When Project Purple did try to reach out via Facebook Messenger, they found many of their messages got stuck in the dreaded "Message Requests," a space on Facebook's design where chats from unknown recipients are stored. Feeling uneasy and uncertain, they needed a partner to help them shore up their social giving strategy.

When we first pitched our solution to Project Purple, their founder Dino Virelli accepted our proposal, but was skeptical. He assumed our solution would operate at a larger scale, but didn't see how it would differ from their previous social tactics. Little did he know the impact it would have on his organization. To build on the energy of Project Purple's in-person events, we decided to host a digital-first Challenge on Facebook. We'll discuss Challenges more later, but know that it's a socially empowered fundraising campaign hosted exclusively on Facebook. Through our knowledge of Meta's social giving tools and Facebook's overall ecosystem, we ran Facebook Ads to get potential supporters to sign up for the month-long running challenge.

After a participant signed up for the challenge, they were encouraged to join a Facebook Group where they could share their own stories, their progress, and why they supported Project Purple in their mission. These Facebook Groups were moderated by hand-picked supporters and Project Purple staff who ensured participants logged their running progress stimulated conversation among the group and answered questions as they arose. These moderators also requested that participants opt-in to Messenger updates. This allowed them to deliver real-time personalized messaging to connect these participants to the organization. Even after the challenge, Project Purple kept the conversation going with their donor base to continue these important relationships.

After about six months of the challenge, we met with Project Purple to review our social giving strategy's progress and its success. Through this strategy, Project Purple not only saw some of its best months of fundraising in eleven years but also cultivated a community of digital supporters that rivaled their in-person events. With just two Challenges on Facebook, Project Purple raised over $120,000 for the fight against pancreatic cancer. And these donations weren't just one-time clicks. They came from the supported community that Project Purple had created on Facebook. For one Project Purple ambassador, these Challenges on Facebook Groups gave her a deeper appreciation for her community of fellow Project Purple supporters.

This supporter, who will remain nameless, had always volunteered for Project Purple's in-person events to honor her late aunt, a victim of pancreatic cancer. She participated in walks and runs across the country whenever she was able. Despite her many years of support, however, she never felt connected to her fellow volunteers at these events. Participants might meet up before the run, she explained, but maintaining a connection afterward was nearly impossible. With the Challenge on Facebook, however, everything was different. By learning from and sharing with all the other Challenge participants, she felt herself grow closer to her digital "marathon" colleagues. When asked about the Project Purple Challenge on Facebook, she revealed, "I've finally found something where my hard work, my miles, my fundraising [feels like] I'm actually making a difference. My aunt's battle ended, but I feel like I took over where she left off."

Project Purple first pursued a social giving strategy as a risk they felt they needed to take to keep everything afloat. This risk, however, gave way to a reward that shot them to new heights. Social giving provided a sustainable new revenue stream born out of the work of an engaged and supportive community. With a greater insight into their donor base, and deeper connections with their most ardent supporters, this first year of record-breaking fundraising numbers was destined to not be their last. After working with GoodUnited, founder Dino Virelli had only one new problem—determining how much of the budget the board would allocate for their social giving strategy. About Project Purple's partnership with us, he mentioned: "[GoodUnited has] allowed us to connect with some really, really amazing strangers who want to help our cause, our mission, and help people at their darkest of times fighting this disease."

Keeping It On Channel

One of the biggest strengths of social giving is that it takes place in the channel where donors are already spending their time. What we mean by "in the channel" is that the fundraiser is hosted completely on Facebook. From creating the fundraiser, to clicking on the donate button, to receiving a thank you message for their donation, the donor's entire experience takes place in the same digital space—

Facebook. The reason why this is so important is because your donors are spending a majority of their time on social media already. Any sort of behavior that disrupts will threaten to disrupt your donation as well. For example, say you make a Facebook post asking for donations, and the post links to your website where the user can place a donation. In clicking on that link, you've already lost that donation, because you've taken them off-channel. According to a report from HootSuite, the average internet user spends about two-and-a-half hours on social media each day, and Facebook still holds the top spot for the social media platform with the most active daily users.[1] Now compare that with how long your average donor spends on a nonprofit's website, and you'll see why donors prefer to give through social media.

In addition to their captive eyeballs, you also make the donation process incredibly easy on the donor. All it takes is one-click to give. Anyone can set up their own Facebook fundraiser in a matter of seconds. And then, still only seconds later, someone can simply click through to donate. This frictionless experience has resulted in record-breaking donations that we'll cover throughout this book, but it is quickly becoming one of the fastest ways to raise the funds you need. Since Facebook first launched its giving tools in 2017, they have amassed over $7 billion in donations for nonprofits and individual fundraisers,[2] every dollar of which has gone on to help nonprofits in the fight for their cause, whether that be saving precious lives, providing critical support services, or fighting for the rights of those that are underserved. That's right, Facebook takes 0 percent for fees, unlike the 5–10 percent of most fundraising software companies. It's

---

1   Simon Kemp, "Digital 2023: Global overview report," January 2023, https://datare-portal.com/reports/digital-2023-global-overview-report.

2   Facebook, "Coming together to raise $5 billion on Facebook and Instagram," March 2023, https://www.facebook.com/business/news/coming-together-to-raise-5-billion-on-facebook-and-instagram-.

clear: social giving represents a frictionless charity experience that meets donors where they are already spending their time. But not all nonprofits are convinced that social giving is worth their effort.

While some may think this new wave in fundraising is simply a trend, social giving is in no way a flash in the pan. In fact, with more and more people spending time on social media, social giving could become the preferred method of giving for the next generation of givers. Now, we know that nonprofits aren't often early adopters, but in the case of social giving, this could spell their doom. Maria Clark, senior vice president at GoodUnited, cited the need for nonprofits to begin "future-proofing" their organizations by diversifying their revenue sources and embracing entrepreneurship after the COVID-19 pandemic. In her article for AFP Global, she challenges late adopters, saying, "it takes investment to build new revenue streams—both time and resources—so don't wait until you 'have to.'"[3] Additionally, Facebook themselves clearly see the value in social giving as these fundraisers keep eyes on their site. To encourage social giving, they've even done away with any transaction fee, making it free for nonprofits to use their fundraising tools.

> Social giving represents a frictionless charity experience that meets donors where they are already spending their time.

Social giving is a new paradigm for philanthropy. It not only brings in a whole new revenue stream for your cause, it also allows

---

3   Marcia Clark, "The future of fundraising: How to future-proof nonprofit fundraising in an uncertain environment," January 2022, https://afpglobal.org/news/future-fundraising-how-future-proof-nonprofit-fundraising-uncertain-environment.

your supporters to be directly involved with your cause. What's more, it expands your donor audience into new untapped potential donors. If you're ready to embrace social giving in your nonprofit's fundraising strategy, we're glad to show you the best path forward for your organization. Throughout this book, we'll provide you tools that will ensure your social fundraising strategy is built to last. And at the end of every chapter, Nick will provide his no-nonsense fundraising tips to help you keep the engine of your fundraising running strong.

Keep in mind that, as a new form of fundraising, social giving is always evolving. It might seem overwhelming at first, and may be challenging depending on your existing social media strategy. By incorporating the lessons of this book, however, you lay a strong foundation that will fortify your nonprofit's fundraising potential. Success all comes down to understanding how this strategy fits into your overall fundraising goals. To understand how your donors will give through this future-proof fundraising method, however, it may be best to look back at the history of philanthropy and why we love to give to nonprofits.

Nick's Tips

- Do an audit of your own organization's social media strategy. How are you soliciting donations on your social channels?

- Consider the experience of your donors on social media. Are you causing friction that may impact their donations?

- Apply for Facebook Fundraising tools. It's simple. It's fast. And it can help you unlock new opportunities for reaching your fundraising goals.

CHAPTER TWO

Why We Give

Humans love to give. Whether giving their time to volunteer in a neighborhood cleanup, purchasing cans of food for a food drive, or donating money to a worthy GoFundMe, charity is a fundamental part of our humanity. There's even evidence of giving that dates back as far as ancient Egypt, where tombs were inscribed with names of people who charitably gave bread and clothes. These inscriptions were the ancient equivalent of getting your name on a park bench plaque as a thank you. Philanthropy is so core to a well-functioning society that ancient Greeks valued it above almost all else. As long as someone has needed help, there's always been someone else willing to help out. When we know we can make a difference, we feel compelled to give to those in need.

But where does this drive come from? Part of it might be just how our brains evolved. When we give, we get a hit of dopamine—one of several pleasure chemicals that float through our brains.[4] Scientists

---

4   Alex Palmer," A neuroscientist explains why it's better to give than to receive," Discover magazine, December 22, 2021, https://www.discovermagazine.com/mind/a-neuroscientist-explains-why-its-better-to-give-than-to-receive.

found that more of our brain lights up when we choose more altruistic choices like philanthropy over selfish gains. Turns out, "it is better to give than to receive" isn't just something your mom told you around Christmas time. Giving is like a drug. It feels good, and the more we give, the better we feel.

The act of giving also builds a community. When we give to a charity we care about, we're immediately connected to those who share our interests. Think about charity runs or a street cleaning day. In those group activities, people with similar backgrounds and experiences connect with each other over the task at hand. By giving back, they create support systems that they can rely on. Take Relay for Life, for example. Started in 1985, this important fundraising event began when one cancer survivor, Dr. Gordon Klatt, wanted to raise awareness and funds for cancer research. To do so, he spent twenty-four hours walking the track at his local university. Relay for Life has now grown into a worldwide movement, with over five thousand relays taking place every year in over twenty countries. At those events, millions of people have come together to provide support, raise money, and work to end cancer.

A goal like ending cancer is indeed lofty, but that's why we are drawn to it. We give because we want to create real change. We want our donation to have an impact—whether that be a month of food for a family in need or mental health services for newly returned vets. When we see that impact, we feel we've closed the loop on our donation. We give, and we see that our donation does something good. Good nonprofits know that their donors want this. To demonstrate impact, they communicate their activity back to their donor base. Whether that's through monthly letters to the donor's house or email newsletters in their inboxes, nonprofits use these kinds of communications to encourage donors to see their impact and to give again. And these kinds of communications work. Research shows that 49 percent of donors are more likely to give again when they learn about the impact of their individual donation. Additionally, 40 percent of donors are more likely to give to a charity after they hear stories about the impact of that organization's work. It's not just that we want to give—we want to know that our giving has made a difference.

So if we all love to give, why is it so taxing on nonprofits to fundraise? Every year, nonprofits collectively pour millions of dollars into campaigns, events, marketing strategies, blog posts, e-blasts, social media, and IT infrastructure to inspire their donor base to contribute to their cause. This takes valuable time and resources away from doing the work the nonprofits were founded to do. While 2021 was a landmark year for charitable giving, it's becoming more difficult for nonprofits to raise the funds they need. And with fundraising activities inspiring fewer donors to give, nonprofits are doing everything in their power to garner their donor's contributions. As we mentioned in the previous chapter, donors are moving away from more traditional methods of fundraising like direct mailers and digital platforms to a more streamlined social experience. Whole new ways of giving make it easier for everyone to donate yet cause complications for traditional fundraising activities.

It's this tension in the nonprofit space that led us to found GoodUnited. In 2012, Nick and I connected over a simple problem—how do we help nonprofits rethink their fundraising strategy and develop a deep community with their donors? Nonprofits are essential to a functioning society, but it's not just because of their altruistic nature. While they do good in pursuit of their mission, they also represent a large portion of our economy. As of 2023, there are over 1.8 million registered nonprofit organizations that account for 5.9 percent of our gross domestic product.[5] Giving isn't just a national pastime; it's a thriving part of our economy that millions of people take part in every day. Our vision is to empower nonprofits to have a one-on-one relationship with every supporter. And yes, we mean *every* supporter.

Too often, nonprofits focus their fundraising efforts on donors who are able to make large-ticket donations. Our GoodUnited cofounder, Nick, finds this tactic to often be extremely disappointing and frustrating. To attract those wealthy donors, he organized a massive fundraising event for his nonprofit, Stop Soldier Suicide. Hosted on the USS Intrepid, the wine-and-cheese affair represented a significant amount of their fundraising budget. He spent thousands to rent out the ship itself. And then there was catering, campaign materials, and a myriad other line items that go into big donor events such as this one. After countless hours planning, the day of the event came. On the ship, Nick worked the room, trying to capture the attention of bankers and other high-yield donors. Yet after the event, he felt exhausted from working so hard for just a few people's donations. He knew there must be a better way to raise the funds he needed to help his fellow service members and veterans.

It wasn't until I met Nick at the University of North Carolina Business School that we found mutual partners in our mission. UNC Business School had felt like the right move after returning from my time with Penny's Way in South Africa. As you may have read in the introduction, I was in the middle of a career transition while in business school. I had been working at several Fortune 500s from IBM to KPMG but I wasn't feeling connected to the work I was doing. It was after spending my sabbatical year volunteering that I began to understand how important nonprofits were to a thriving global

---

5   Independent Sector, "Health of the U.S. nonprofit sector quarterly review," January 2023, https://independentsector.org/resource/health-of-the-u-s-nonprofit-sector.

community. That experience at Penny's Way inspired me to leave the corporate world and set out on my own journey of making a difference for nonprofits. That's where Nick and I joined forces to found GoodUnited, a nonprofit technology company redefining peer-to-peer fundraising. While we've had our successes and our failures, our technology comes back to one fundamental thing—understanding how and why donors give to worthy causes.

How We Used to Give

Today, charitable giving is at an all-time high. In 2020 alone, nonprofits received over $471 billion in charitable contributions. Sixty-nine percent of those donations were given by individual Americans just like you. While the COVID-19 pandemic and the Black Lives Matter movement drove many to give, these numbers are consistent with an annual growth rate of 5.1 percent since 2010. Even amidst the recessions of 2020, people still gave. These contributions show us that giving is recession-proof. It isn't just something we do when we have extra cash lying around. We love to give, and we're not slowing down any time soon. Many nonprofits, however, can't keep up with the pace of their donors, and they're missing out on millions of dollars that could help their organization.

But why is that? Well, fifty years ago, when you wanted to give to a nonprofit, you had two options: donate to a representative of the charity on the street or take your donation directly to their headquarters. In the early days of American fundraising, it was common to see charities take to the streets to directly appeal to pedestrians for contributions. Think Salvation Army and their brigades of bell ringers that continue to this day. Passersby would drop whatever change they had into the charity's bucket, exchange a few kind words, and be on their way. Additionally, representatives from these charities would go door to door asking homeowners if they could contribute anything to their cause. While taxing, these "on-the-street" tactics proved fruitful for many early nonprofits.

The other method required a lot more commitment from the donor. They'd have to head to the local headquarters of their favorite nonprofit—say the YMCA—write a check, hand it to them, and walk out. The donor gets to give, the nonprofits get to receive, and the transaction is complete. While this method was effective, it required a lot of effort from the donor. To increase the frequency of these donations, nonprofits began to collect information on their donors so that they could stay in touch. They began to ask for a donor's mailing address at the time of donation so that they could send follow-up letters to continue the conversation.

With that, nonprofits captured their first data point about their donors: the all-important mailing address. With a record of donor addresses, fundraisers could send direct mailers to their donation base with messages about the nonprofit's mission and pictures of the good work they were doing. They also included an appeal: "If you like the work we're doing, please consider a donation today." And with that request, a handy return mail envelope where the donor could drop a check in the mail back to the nonprofit. This made the donation process easier for the donors. Now, they could send their donation via mail, and never have to leave the comfort of their own home. These direct mailers became a primary fundraising tactic for nonprofits and are still popular today.

With the advent of the internet, however, nonprofits saw a new opportunity for donors. They could capture contributions using their websites and collect even more information about their donors. This made things easier for the donor and for the nonprofit. The donor didn't even need to open an envelope! They just had to open a web browser, navigate to the website, and with a few clicks, a contribution was complete and a thank you email was sent. Additionally, nonprofits could use their donation pages as data collecting tools. Before you donate, you'd have to put in your name, your age, your mailing address, email, phone number, and anything else that the nonprofit thought would be useful in engaging you. With this information, nonprofits built thorough and powerful email lists that allowed them to contact their donor base whenever and wherever. As these digital tactics evolved, they collected more data, which allowed for more targeted messages that captured donors' attention. This shifted power into the hands of nonprofits who continued to evolve their email marketing campaigns to become faster, more specific, and more frequent.

Yet, you only need to open your inbox today to see that these tactics are becoming less effective. How many more times does an elected official need to send out an email with the subject line "THIS IS IT [your name]" or "WE NEED YOUR HELP NOW, [your name]!" before it captures your attention? And how much time do you think you spend, on average, on your favorite nonprofit's website every week? Is it zero hours? Traditional digital platforms like websites are becoming obsolete. Today, we spend most of our time on social media platforms where we post content, connect with each other, buy things, and yes, even donate to our favorite causes.

How We Donate Today

On its surface, it's easy for a nonprofit to see social media as just an additional channel that they can use to engage their users. Some fundraising specialists only see social media as a way to amplify the message and impact of their nonprofit, and point all donors back to their website to collect their contribution. They prefer to focus on growing their subscriber list for their e-blasts and using social media to add to those lists. But that's just not how these donors are using social media, nor is it how these social channels want their donors to use their platforms. To be blunt, it is in Facebook's best interest to keep their users' eyes on Facebook for ad revenue. How does this affect the donor experience? It means all donor activity is operated and owned by Facebook. This makes a sleek experience for the donor, while causing several big problems for nonprofits.

First off, traditional fundraising infrastructure is powered by donor information. Campaigns run on addresses, phone numbers, and emails that connect them to their donor base. Each data point is like a door that leads directly to a donor and unlocks their ability to give again. When a donor gives through a social channel, however, there are no doors, just a mass of contributions that arrive unmarked and unsigned. This is because social media platforms do not uniquely identify individuals who donate or those who create fundraisers. And what little information they do provide is limited and typically doesn't include the all-important fundraiser email that fuels fundraising campaigns. Remember, they want to keep their users on their platforms. Social media channels are only interested in the moment of giving and aren't concerned with opening up opportunities for future donations. When using Facebook to fundraise, nonprofits are unable to leverage their existing IT infrastructure to continue to grow donor relationships.

A benefit for nonprofits in this new age of social giving, however, is that social media platforms have expanded charity into new generations of donors. Many donors who give through social media are first-time donors. Of those who have given through Facebook, 88 percent say they will likely do it again. Social media is where donors are spending most of their time interacting with their friends and family.[6] Nonprofits need to meet them there to grab their attention. Remember, social giving represents $5 billion from individual donors! Nonprofits that ignore this shift not only stand to lose out on massive donations but will miss opportunities to create meaningful relationships with their donors, and an impassioned donor base.

Generally, social media users are digital natives. This means they're savvy when it comes to marketing campaigns and can sense when something feels inauthentic or "salesy." This causes problems for nonprofits who invest in a generic social media strategy. So how are these donors giving? Typically, they donate to a cause that they saw pop up on their timeline from a friend or a family member. Users are also more likely to donate to a cause that is important to their community on social media. While this might feel like the nonprofit is being left in the dark, there's a huge opportunity here for these organizations to become a part of these online communities through targeted messaging. For example, 59 percent of people who engage with nonprofits on social media end up taking some sort of action, such as making a donation, to forward that organization's cause.[7] It's like the community is already there. All these nonprofits need to do is to engage with it.

Stories and user-generated content are the foundation of any good social media platform. Nonprofits can leverage this capability to demonstrate the immediate impact of a donor's contribution. When a nonprofit engages on their social media channels, they have

---

6   "Social media giving statistics for nonprofits," Nonprofits Source, https://nonprof-itssource.com/online-giving-statistics/social-media/#:~:text=Facebook,or%20important%20to%20their%20business.

7   Ben Matthews, "Social media stats for charities and nonprofits," Empower, June 2022, https://empower.agency/social-media-stats-charities-nonprofits/.

the opportunity to tell a powerful story that illustrates their cause or mission. Animal shelters are a great example of this. Who doesn't want to see a picture of a formerly sheltered dog now living a happy life with his new adopted parents? Oh, and if you want to see this happen for more dogs, you can always donate or volunteer. With the press of the giving button on a nonprofit's page, the transaction becomes almost too easy to resist. For those that donate online, 25 percent say social media is the communication channel that most inspires them to give.[8] These stories are all over social media, and they drive donors to action.

> When a nonprofit engages on their social media channels, they have the opportunity to tell a powerful story that illustrates their cause or mission.

Finally, social media democratizes giving. While you might not be able to collect every piece of a donor's information, you are given a small window into their world through a social media's chat function. That's right—get into those DMs! By sending the right message to the right donor at the right time, you can thank them for their donation, better understand how they view your organization, and inquire after future donations. This direct conversation (done well) encourages the donor. They not only feel like their contribution matters to the organization, they see themselves in the organization's mission. We've found that, when nonprofits directly message their donors on Facebook, the open rate is over 90 percent! This is an

---

8   Nonprofit Tech for Good, "2020 Global trends in giving report," January 2021. https://www.nptechforgood.com/2020/09/14/newly-released-the-2020-global-trends-in-giving-report/#:~:text=55%25%20of%20donors%20worldwide%20prefer,in%20a%20recurring%20giving%20program.

unheard-of rate in the world of email marketing. These huge open rates result in a campaign collecting upward of twenty times more revenue from conversational messaging than they would have in their normal fundraising activities.

The benefits for nonprofits who successfully track and engage their in-channel donations far outweigh the issues it causes for legacy fundraising activity. GoodUnited was founded to empower nonprofits to take advantage of this new shift and reap the benefits for their cause. Our product tracks fundraisers on social media platforms, providing nonprofits unprecedented insights into donor behavior. Equipped with this information, nonprofit leaders can deepen their connection with their donors simply by sending them a direct message. Over the last three years, GoodUnited has helped nonprofits raise over $1B on Facebook. For many of these donors, in-channel giving was the first time they donated to a cause. Our product enables nonprofits to connect with a fundraising base that was previously unavailable to them.

In building this tool, our team has learned a lot about how and why people support their favorite causes. Since 2014, we've seen donor behavior evolve from direct mailers to e-blasts to birthday fundraisers and beyond. While we started as a newsletter designed to collect donor information for our nonprofit clients, we quickly realized the importance of in-channel donation. By the end of 2020, we'd worked with hundreds of nonprofits on their social fundraising solutions. Have we always succeeded? Absolutely not. But we've grown from those mistakes. Our hearts, our minds, and our hands are dedicated to this mission. We have a passion for helping those who help others.

Leaders of nonprofits (like maybe yourself) have enough to deal with in the day-to-day operations of their organization. They shouldn't have to fret over every aspect of their annual fundraising strategy. At GoodUnited, we want to show you, nonprofit leader, that there's an easier and more effective way to fundraise. And no, we don't mean get rid of your direct mailers. In our work in this space, we've seen what tactics are effective with which donors. The first step is to gain a clear understanding of your donor base— their motivations, passions, and needs. That's why we're writing this book: to provide you with strategies that can assist you and your team in your fundraising activities. We've helped multiple big-ticket nonprofits garner millions in donations, and we can do it for you too. The work you do is too important to not receive the support it deserves. Let us show you how you can capture that and more.

> **The work you do is too important to not receive the support it deserves.**

Nick's Tips

- Donor behavior has changed as new technological advances arise. By investing in your social giving strategy today, you lay a solid foundation for the next innovation in giving.

- Social giving is an additional arm of your overall fundraising strategy. While you shouldn't only rely on e-blasts, make sure that your social giving strategy is in harmony with the rest of your tactics.

- Social media allows people to share their stories of giving to their network. By harnessing the power of these stories, your nonprofit can expand into new audiences of donors.

CHAPTER THREE

Starting the Conversation

At fundraising events for Stop Soldier Suicide like the one I mentioned on the USS Intrepid, Nick spends 95 percent of his time talking to the donors that support the cause. When he started the organization, these conversations felt like those awkward moves you make when you meet someone for the first time. You know this kind of chat. You don't know a lot about the other person, so you ask probing questions in hopes you'll discover some shared interest between the two of you. After that first conversation, maybe you have another, and before you know it, you've made a real connection with someone. That personal connection is invaluable for nonprofits. When you have that with a member of your donor base, you know you can rely on their continued support. Even though it can feel uncomfortable, you must make that first move.

That's why Nick treats that donor at the fundraising party like anyone else he's just meeting. He takes the time to ask the questions that give him a fuller picture of that person. From this conversation, he wants to learn as much about this potential donor as he can. He wants to know what their hobbies are, how many kids they have, what kind of car they drive—anything that colors in a bit more of the mental picture he's building of them in his head. When he feels he knows enough about this person, he moves to act. He gets down to the reason why he started the conversation in the first place. That final question usually goes like this:

"Look, I just want to say thank you for your donations. Can I ask why you gave to Stop Soldier Suicide today?" This is the most important piece of information he needs. It's why Nick has hosted the event that they are both attending, held on a gorgeous rooftop in Arlington, Virginia, as the sun sets on the Potomac. You see, Nick knows that he shares one common interest with his donors: they both want to see service members get the mental health resources they need. If these donors know their contribution was critical to accomplishing that mission, they would feel like they've made a difference. The personal relationship they have with Nick adds another layer. These donors now see him as a partner in their personal mission to help service members. But if he doesn't engage them as a real person, they might not think their donation is valued by the organization and they may withdraw their support. Having this kind of relationship with your donors means you must stay *in* conversations with them or you risk losing them.

Seasoned fundraisers are familiar with this kind of donor chit-chat. In fact, many nonprofit organizations have whole wings of their institutions dedicated to these wine-and-cheese conversations. The funds raised through donor relations is sometimes the reason nonprofits can pay the bills and do their work. But caring for a worthy cause isn't reserved for the wealthy who can afford to attend these events. According to the Tax Policy Center, folks making under $50,000 a year give away a higher percentage of their annual salary than almost every income bracket.[9] These are the kinds of folks you'd more likely catch at your local grocery store than a high-ticket gala event. You see, everyone wants to support the causes they care about, regardless of their annual income. But fundraisers are already stretched thin by making moves with their highest donors. They can't have a deep conversation with every single one of our supporters—right?

Many nonprofit organizations think that having a relationship with every single donor is just not scalable. There are just too many people who give! By the end of 2022, 1.4 billion people worldwide had donated money to nonprofit organizations.[10] To have just a five-minute conversation with each of those people would take over thirty thousand years! Suffice to say, no one—not even nonprofit professionals—has that kind of time. So, they rely on their mass forms of communication, like e-blasts and mailers, to stay in touch with their donor base. But these forms hardly inspire a deep relationship. Mailers sit in a donor's mailbox wedged between bills and junk mail inspiring no loyalty. E-blasts, while more immediate than mailers, are maybe the most impersonal form of communication. With this in mind, who can blame fundraisers who spend their time deepening the relationships with the donors with the deepest pockets? They're betting on the sure thing that will keep their organization funded. For them, engaging the rest of their base may not give them the returns

---

9   Tax Policy Center Briefing Book, August 2018, https://www.taxpolicycenter.org/briefing-book.

10   Nonprofit Source, "Charitable giving statistics for 2023," January 2023, https://non-profitssource.com/online-giving-statistics/.

they need. And, with their operating budgets on the line, they just aren't willing to take that risk.

With social media, however, nonprofits can speak directly to large numbers of people who care deeply about their cause. Facebook, Instagram, TikTok, and the host of new platforms that are being developed each day allow people, businesses, and organizations to connect. Almost since the first Facebook status was liked, the for-profit world has taken full advantage of these connections to sell products and turn followers into brand evangelists. Nonprofits, however, have always thought of a dedicated social media strategy as a "nice-to-have." It's an advocacy tool to spread the message of their cause and not a vital part of their fundraising efforts. We know, however, that social giving is changing how we support the causes we care most about.

For an example of this shift, let me tell you about one of our earliest clients: Best Friends Animal Society, an animal welfare group. We helped them create and enact a social media strategy that would bring them closer to their most earnest supporters. Halfway through their fundraising campaign, they got a direct message from one of their social media followers. Through this DM, we saw that it was an elderly lady who was one of Best Friends' most devoted supporters. For the past few years, she had been using Facebook to raise funds for Best Friends on her birthday. It was through these Facebook birthday fundraisers that she became more involved with Best Friends Animal Society. Through her work fundraising for the organization, she began to see Best Friends' mission to care for animals as her own. And, in her message to us, she shared that she wished for her work to go on without her.

"It has been so wonderful raising funds for [Best Friends] in the past," she said in the DM. "I have decided that I'd like to name your organization as a beneficiary in my will. Could you help me get that set up?" In that message, we knew that there was a shift happening. This generous lady felt so connected to the Best Friends mission that she wanted to support them even after she was gone. When you look at the hierarchy of what nonprofits want to achieve, a supporter naming your organization as a beneficiary is right at the top. This exchange was the catalyst for us to start looking deep into in-app messaging as a way to create authentic connections between nonprofits and their supporters.

Building one-on-one relationships with your supporters *is* possible through social media and the opportunities it provides. Through social media's Messenger platform, you're able to open up a window directly to your supporters and start conversations with them. In that conversation, you will learn about these supporters—their motivations and interests. If you ask the right questions, you'll learn how they're connected to your cause. You can use social media to thank them for their support and encourage them to continue. Social media makes it easy so that you can make moves with every single one of your supporters. And with social fundraising tools that allow users to crowdsource funds on birthdays, anniversaries, and other important dates, a new type of nonprofit supporter is emerging: the Social Fundraiser.

The Social Fundraiser

The social fundraiser is your not-so-secret weapon in this third shift toward social giving. You might already have some of these kinds of people following you on your socials. These aren't just the people who hit "like" on your Facebook page. They are the ones who go out of their way to make posts about their connection to your cause. They have a personal connection to your cause. They're the people who care so much that they're willing to go out of their way to raise money from their friends and family on social media to forward your organization's mission. They urge their followers to donate whatever they can to your organization because they know that the work your organization does is invaluable. They are more than just supporters. They're partners in your mission, and they're going to help you accomplish it.

> The social fundraiser is your not-so-secret weapon in this third shift toward social giving.

And, like I said, maybe you already have these zealous supporters who want to raise funds for you. That's great! But have you talked to them one-on-one? A good nonprofit uses their social media presence to share resources and spread awareness. An exceptional nonprofit uses their social pages to speak directly to their community. Tools developed to help are built into the platform. Using groups in Facebook, you can put yourself right in the middle of conversations that are already being had about your cause. And with Facebook Messenger, you can create a dialogue with the individuals who contribute the most. Using these social tools, you can build a network to raise cumulative funds year after year. You just have to know how to use them.

To get a better understanding of these social tools, I want to tell you about one of our biggest clients: Susan G. Komen. As one of the leading breast cancer organizations in the world, they fight breast cancer on multiple fronts from community engagement to in-the-lab work. Since their founding in 1982, Komen has raised over $2.9 billion in funds for cancer research, community health outreach, and advocacy for public policy. Through these funds, they support community programs for survivors and families in over sixty countries. For over three decades, supporters, survivors, and organizers alike have come together under Komen's umbrella to advocate for a cure for breast cancer and remember those who have lost their lives to it. Their strong network of supporters made this important work possible.

When we first started working with Komen in 2018, they felt there was more that they could do with their community. With over two million followers on Facebook, Komen's Facebook page had a lot of traffic. Very little of that attention, however, translated to funds raised. They used their presence to provide information, advertise volunteering opportunities, and remind their followers about breast health. But that's where their engagement ended. Meanwhile, in the comments, their fans were having robust conversations about breast health–sharing experiences and supporting each other in their fights with cancer. Komen was just the platform for these back-and-forths between their followers. To take the next step, they would need to make a first move of their own.

With the boom in social giving, Facebook has created a suite of tools for nonprofits to use in their fundraising activities. We've worked with Meta, the company that owns and operates Facebook and Instagram, several times to leverage these tools to help our clients maximize their raised funds. We believe that if these technologies help multinational corporations make billions, why shouldn't they do the same for nonprofits working toward worthy causes? So, we turned to Facebook Messenger to begin the conversation with Komen's supporters.

We saw that Komen's followers on Facebook were already raising funds for the organization through social giving. Yet, in many of these instances, a user would crowdsource funds for their birthday one year and then wouldn't the next. In those 365 days, they forgot about Komen and the work they had supported through their birthday on

Facebook. Perhaps they felt underappreciated, or they just forgot. Regardless, this meant that funds that were there for Komen one year were not there the next. We needed to find a way to get these users to raise funds over multiple years. For Komen's social strategy, we implemented a solution to appreciate and coach all of their fundraisers. This turnkey solution allows the Komen foundation to personally thank and coach every supporter on Facebook who creates a birthday, or honorarium fundraiser on its behalf.

Let's say that Sarah, one of Komen's followers, raises funds for the organization on her birthday. The Appreciate and Coach service would follow up with a direct message to Sarah that thanked her for her work and asked her if she'd like help fundraising. After starting this conversation with Sarah, the tool would continue to engage her in conversation. Through these DMs, Komen could coach Sarah with fundraising tips and tricks, specific calls to action, and useful resources from Komen. With this tool, Komen can show appreciation for Sarah's work, maximize her ability to fundraise, and build the foundation of a relationship with Sarah, someone who may not have crowdfunded without encouragement.

Through this conversation with Sarah in that Messenger window, Komen brings Sarah into the organization. These few chat bubbles invite an ardent supporter of the cause into an institution who's made that cause their mission. And it doesn't stop there. We can learn even more about Sarah by asking Nick's favorite fundraising gala question: *"Sarah, Can I ask you why you donated today?"* That's how we learn Sarah's mom lost her battle with breast cancer. In fact, Sarah chose to raise funds for Komen because her mom took part in the Tour de Komen, an annual 100-mile cycling Komen fundraising event. She became familiar with Komen because, an avid cyclist herself, she joined her mom on one of these rides. What started off as a simple fundraising question revealed a lot about who Sarah is. We learn what motivates her, what her hobbies are, and how she's connected to Komen's cause.

Now, multiply that by Komen's two million Facebook followers and you can see how conversational messaging can turn loyal supporters into a trusted network of social fundraisers willing to give you their discretionary effort. Each participant can also choose how much they want to be involved. By asking if they want to maintain contact with Komen, these supporters can sign up for ongoing messages in Messenger where they will be reminded of important campaigns in Komen's fundraising calendar. Supporters who opted in to this service were two times more likely to click through to Komen's main page than those who hadn't subscribed. This increased paged traffic translated directly into an increase in funds raised. Based on GoodUnited's data from A/B testing, we know that those who opt into year-round messages raise more on average for Komen.

These conversations were miles away from the one-way updates their social page used to be. "We aren't just broadcasting one way," says Melody Boatwright, Komen's vice president of Integrated Marketing. "We have this amazing opportunity to get to know our supporters, tailor our messages to them, express our gratitude, and keep them informed through year-round messages." Messages also asked members how they would like to participate with the Komen foundation. Representatives from Komen would offer other ways to get involved such as advocacy, volunteering, or attending a Komen event. In their individual chats, they'd present members with targeted events that seemed most in line with their interest. Sarah, for example, might receive word about a cycling event that Komen is throwing that's near her home.

The Susan G. Komen foundation used two-way social messaging to transform their in-person engagement into a thriving online community that helped them raise funds. Through these tools, they coached over thirty-seven thousand social fundraisers to raise $2 million for cancer research and advocacy. And their social media blew up as well. Their Facebook page reach doubled, enlarging their audience to new folks who wanted to join in their fight against cancer. The folks at Komen saw the power of having a one-on-one relationship with each of their donors and reaped the benefits of the emerging world of social giving. As their reach grew, however, new problems arose that caused them to shift their approach from the individual to the group. We'll follow up with their approach to these changing issues in the next chapter.

Starting Your Conversations

What we can learn from Komen is that an "engaged community" doesn't always translate to funds raised. While they had millions of followers, their social channels didn't speak with their followers as individuals. In this new era of charitable giving, starting these conversations is the first step in creating that engaged nonprofit community of social fundraisers. This means more funds for your cause, which means you can continue in your organization's larger mission. By starting conversations with your donors, understanding their motivations, and leveraging off-the-shelf social tools, you can take advantage of this new mode of fundraising and successfully reach your fundraising goals.

First, *start the conversations* with your donors through in-app messaging wherever they are most active. Do you have thousands of followers on your Facebook page? Great! What have you done with them? When you just update your followers through status and posts, you're creating one-way conversations that end before you even post them. Figure out who's the most engaged in your online community—it's probably those folks who have crowdsourced funds for your cause. Take the time to thank them for what they've done for your cause. With these first few moves, you've already got an opening to take the next step in building a relationship with them.

The next step of any relationship is to gain *a deeper understanding* of the other person. So, ask your social fundraisers *"why did you donate to our cause today?"* This open-ended question establishes a two-way conversation with your supporter. By letting them answer however they'd like, you get a snapshot of this person and how they view your cause. Your supporter learns that you care about what they have to say. Through further inquiry, you can come to know what they care about, how they spend their time, and how they want to be involved in your cause. With this valuable data, you can further personalize your conversation with them and offer ways to connect with your organization that best suits them.

And you may be thinking: *This is too much! How am I going to find the time to talk to every single one of our donors?* That's why we *leverage existing social tools* to reach our supporters. Meta has a suite of tools that are specifically designed for nonprofit organizations to reach and engage the supporters of their cause. Sending messages year-round is one effective tip. There are also other tactics to help you manage the data you get from your conversations and tailor the messages you send to your supporters. There are even tools outside of Meta's suite that could help you in your mission. ChatFuel is a great, affordable option that manages your social conversations. Regardless, remember there are tools out there that you can use to your advantage.

We continue to work with Komen to this day to help them sustain the relationships they've built with their donor base. The way they've built and maintained their community over the years stands as an example to many nonprofits who are just starting out. While we've talked a lot about how fundraising keeps your organization going, let me be clear about one thing. It's not money that fuels a nonprofit. It's not even their mission that keeps them going. It's the community they build around their cause. The people that they touch through their work have the power to sustain them in their massively important work. Because when budgets aren't funded, and programs are being shut down, what else do you have but your community?

> It's not money that fuels a nonprofit. It's not even their mission that keeps them going. It's the community they build around their cause.

Nick's Tips

- To best understand your donor base, take the time to first identify your most zealous supporters—your Social Fundraisers—and thank them for their help in your cause.

- Gain a deeper understanding of your supporters by engaging them on the channels that they are most active. This invites them into your cause and your organization.

- Use existing social tools to help you succeed with your social giving strategy.

CHAPTER FOUR

Empower Your Supporters to Fundraise for You

Kayleigh Thomas

This year, instead of sending me a Happy Birthday message, I'm asking you to contribute to Susan G. Komen to help them continue to fight for cancer survivors everywhere.

 143   45 comments

Andrew Welch

It's been a year since my son passed, and in honor of his life, please consider donating to Stop Soldier Suicide so they can get resources into the hands of our service members battling through their darkest moments.

 116   79 comments

 Jenny Jenkins

Today is my daughter's first day of elementary school, and to celebrate, would you consider sending some money to No Kid Hungry? Every kid deserves to go to school without feeling hungry and it's their mission to get food to every kid in need.

 89   24 comments

You probably see messages like these every day on your Facebook feed. Social fundraising now means anyone can crowdsource funds for you. These personalized fundraisers connect your most ardent supporters to your nonprofit's cause. When they raise funds for your organization, your supporters make your cause their own. They chose your organization because it fits within their own personal mission and motivations.

Yet the nonprofit has no control when their social fundraisers start these micro-crowdfunding campaigns or how these campaigns are run. Social giving tools, as they currently stand, provide little more than a check to the nonprofit at the moment of donation. They don't track donor information, and what little information they do have, they don't share back with the nonprofits. This means that nonprofits can do little more than accept the donation and move on. Some nonprofits see this as passive on their part. How can they influence people on an individual level to give? For this reason, these nonprofit leaders discount social giving entirely.

What these nonprofit leaders fail to recognize about social giving is the *social* aspect of these fundraisers. Social fundraisers are blasting their nonprofit's message across their Facebook feeds, but because they think it is too difficult to manage, they're not willing to take the time to harness this energy. Handled properly, however, nonprofits can encourage the momentum behind these one-off fundraising campaigns. By leveraging the interpersonal aspect of social giving, they're able to expand into new donor populations and engage a strong army of supporters for your cause. And the solution lies in understanding your donor's motivations and little old-fashioned competition.

Turning the Flywheel

Peer-to-peer crowdfunding campaigns are a flywheel in your fundraising where you harness the power of your strongest supporters. While these engaged supporters are using their birthdays to raise funds for you, they're also amplifying the message of your organization to their friends and family. And with the frictionless experience provided through Facebook's social giving tools, those who contribute are able to do so without leaving the platform. While these one-off crowdfunding instances may seem unpredictable, they are a spark that expands your brand to reach new donor populations. It's up to you, however, to encourage that spark to flame. To do that, you must understand these dedicated supporters and learn how to build on their momentum.

People get on Facebook because they want to feel like they belong. They post updates, comment on posts, and join groups because they want to stay in touch with their inner circle. According to a report developed in collaboration with HootSuite, 71 percent of respondents said they use Facebook primarily to communicate with their friends and family.[11] When choosing what brands and pages to interact with on Facebook, users consider what message that sends to their social circles. Choosing to like a politician or a nonprofit, for example, sends a message to their followers. They expect the brands they interact with on social media to share their values and to act on those values. In another study, over 70 percent of respondents claimed they wanted brands to speak out on social issues, with 41 percent saying they expect these brands to actively engage in listening to their communities.[12] People get on Facebook because they want to feel like a part of a community, and they want the organizations they *like* to join in that as well.

To best utilize your social strategy, you must create a community around your nonprofit's cause on your social platforms. One place to start is by forging connections between the social fundraisers that have already committed to your mission and raised funds for your cause. Historically, nonprofits did this by hosting big fundraising events like marathons and food drives. These in-person events provide volunteering opportunities for folks invested in the nonprofit's cause. American Cancer Society's Relay for Life, for example, has become a locus of action where lifelong supporters can connect over shared experiences

---

11   Simon Kemp, "Digital 2022 July global statshot," Kepios LTD, July 2022, https://datareportal.com/reports/digital-2022-july-global-statshot.

12   Sprout Social, "U.S. social media trends for 2022."

and passions. Yet, as the COVID-19 pandemic taught us, we can't rely solely on in-person events to create these moments for connection. Not to mention, many of these events are held in specific locations. Your nonprofit may have supporters in parts of the country where you aren't hosting fundraising events.

Then how do you engage with all of your donors without spreading your event budget too thin? During the COVID-19 pandemic, we have seen many industries shift from in-person events to remote events that connect people from around the world. On-demand streaming took over the gap left from empty movie theaters. Online shopping replaced our afternoon shopping trips. Concerts that were scheduled in large venues moved to digital-only events for diehard fans. And while this was not always enjoyable, industries adapted to the new normal. Now, nonprofits can learn from this shift.

Post-COVID, socially native fundraising has emerged as the prominent new fundraising method. With digital-first fundraising events, you establish a strong new community of supporters. When your supporters are boosting your nonprofit's signal, you have the potential to ride their enthusiasm and attract new donors and supporters to your cause. Through social fundraising events, your nonprofit can experience the best of two worlds in one solution—peer-to-peer encouragement and social media virality. The best method for this that we at GoodUnited have found are Challenges on Facebook. These social campaigns are the perfect way to connect with your social supporters and encourage them to continue their support of your cause.

A Facebook Challenge is a time-bound, social fundraising–based, peer-to-peer campaign fully conducted in-channel on Facebook. During a Challenge, participants complete a specified activity while raising funds for your nonprofit on Facebook. They use videos and posts about their activity to ask their followers to contribute to your nonprofit's cause. To connect with other supporters, Challenge participants join a Facebook group created specifically for the event. Through Challenges, you're able to grow your community of supporters and take advantage of the enthusiasm of your most committed fans.

To illustrate the power of these social campaigns, let's break down an example Facebook Challenge. Say a nonprofit starts a thirty-day plank challenge where participants commit to doing one thirty-second plank every day. Every day, participants are asked to track their progress and share their plank video on their socials. While doing so, they create a Facebook fundraiser where their followers donate to their goal with one click. Throughout the month, other plank participants share their experience of their own workout plan in a Challenge participant group. It's in this group where they can meet folks who share at least two of their interests: planking and their passion for that nonprofit's cause. Because of that support system, these supporters raise more money for your nonprofit than they would alone.

These Challenges can also expand into new groups of supporters through Facebook Ads. Nonprofits can create a set of ads with keywords that promote the Challenge to users outside of their traditional audience. These keywords can be around the activity—"plank" or "abs" for the prior example—or around a specific demographic—"military" or "service-members" to attract folks for Stop Soldier Suicide. This pushes the Challenge out to a broader community like people who are interested in the activity component for whom your cause is just an added benefit. By using these digital-first events, nonprofits can reach new supporters who might not have engaged with an in-person event. At the end of those thirty days, the nonprofit not only has an additional fundraising avenue in social giving, but it also has a new bench of supporters ready to help the cause.

Let's be clear: social fundraising challenges aren't new. Charitable marathons and telethons, for example, have brought in millions of dollars for nonprofits over the years. They even share some similarities with Facebook Challenges. Viral activities like the Ice Bucket Challenge, which had a huge impact on funding for ALS research, were powered by social media for one example. Unfortunately, the challenge predates Facebook's fundraising tools, and nonprofits that fight ALS could not take advantage of these tools' benefits. But this proves that people love to give when they know there is a social element. Whether it's a 5k run or dunking their heads in ice-cold water, raising money is fun when competition is involved. Some nonprofit organizations, however, worry that Facebook Challenges cannibalize their established and popular in-person events.

In fact, they do not. These digital-first Challenge events are an additive fundraising method for nonprofits looking to take advantage of the expansion in social giving. Through our time working in this space, we've seen that nonprofits are more likely to attract new participants through Facebook Challenges than they would with an in-person event. To continue the momentum of this engaged digital community, these Challenges can also be easily repeated for several months, allowing it to be a part of a larger fundraising campaign. Finally, the low acquisition costs of these events build your donor file in a more cost-effective way. In essence, it's easy to set up, it builds your brand, it creates an excited community, and it raises serious funds for your cause. All this for a fraction of the price of in-person events. To highlight the power of Facebook Challenges, let's look at an organization that turned to these digital-first events when the rest of the world went dark.

American Cancer Society and Facebook Challenges

At GoodUnited, the first time we understood the true potential of Facebook Challenges was when we worked with the American Cancer Society in early 2020. Every year, ACS holds their biggest fundraiser, Relay for Life, the most popular peer-to-peer fundraising event for the last thirty-five years. With over two thousand local events across the country, millions have participated in walks in their communities to bring an end to this debilitating disease. Since ACS held their first walk, Relay for Life has raised over $6 billion for the organization. These contributions have funded important research studies, provided support for patients and survivors, and fueled the never-ending fight against cancer. Relay for Life was a prime part of ACS's fundraising portfolio.

At the beginning of the COVID pandemic, however, social distancing restrictions prevented ACS from hosting these events that were vital to their organization. For the first time in the history of the organization, they had to make a decision—find a new way to raise over $300 million. Without these funds, important research initiatives for the fight against cancer were at stake. At this point, GoodUnited had already partnered with ACS to maximize their social fundraising on Facebook. When it was official that Relay for Life would be on hold, however, they turned to us to understand how they could pivot to digital-first events to fill the gap that COVID had caused.

"We realized that we needed to lead with a digital-first mindset to drive revenue, and engage donors," the national vice president for Relay for Life said. While the folks at ACS had deep experience in in-person fundraising events, they had only a short time to research, lay out, and execute a social fundraising plan that centered around digital-first events. While they encouraged their supporters to create

Facebook fundraisers through their event websites, only a quarter followed through. Like many organizations, ACS needed to understand how they could host a digital experience that inspired the same excitement, motivation, and passion as Relay for Life.

The question stood: how could ACS emulate the same excitement and engagement that inspired people during Relay for Life? Together with ACS, we began to dive into what made Relay for Life so popular. What we discovered was that it was two things: the physical activity of walking and the community built around the walk. That's when we thought maybe the walk wasn't off after all. With Facebook Challenges, we could effectively have participants do the walk on their own terms and at their own pace. As a pilot, we ran Facebook Ads for a one-month Challenge for ACS. The ads targeted people in three locations. Those who signed up were then put into Facebook Groups with other folks from their region. Each group also was assigned a different physical activity—walking, running, doing squats—to track over the next month.

Through these Facebook Challenge groups, participants shared their stories with each other. They commiserated on the difficulty of their physical challenge and through that grew closer. They talked about whether they had supported ACS or not and for how long. Participants shared events that they had attended, and others would comment, "I was there! Did I see you there?" And they made new connections. For some participants, this digital-first Walk for Life was their first ACS event. Thanks to ads that grabbed their attention, they felt compelled to join the challenge and grow the ACS community. Through the Challenge group, they learned more about ACS and its mission. ACS even got involved in the conversation, posting weekly topics to spark the conversation and commenting with resources where necessary.

Within the challenge group, a real community was growing that mimicked the flows of the one created by the in-person versions of Relay for Life. Participants encouraged each other to hit their exercise goals throughout the challenge period. They offered each other tips to increase their fundraising potential. And they even were able to share the load for others when it seemed too tough. Posts like the one below were common in the Challenge groups:

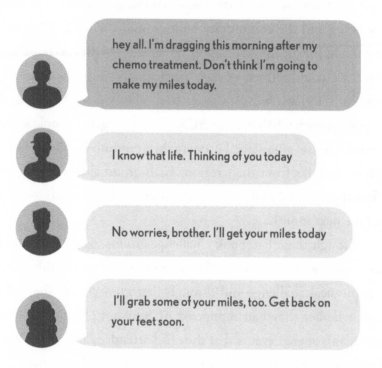

Participants cheered for each other in these groups. They listened to each other's complaints and celebrations. Through post after post, you can see this group that were once strangers become a community that looks out for each other. The only difference between the digital event and the in-person event was the location of the participants.

Until this point, social fundraising through Facebook birthdays was a one-way transaction. A user would post their Facebook fundraiser. Their friends would donate. And then, at the end of the fundraiser, the donations would go to the nonprofit. Through these multiple funnel points, nonprofits could see the support coming in, but it lacked the community culture that we expect from a social experience. With Challenges, however, nonprofits cast a wide net into their social channels to catch new supporters of their cause. Then, by encouraging group culture, the connections between your supporters multiply. That one-way connection to your organization branches out to the many individuals who care for your cause.

The financial support that poured in from the ACS Facebook Challenges was unbelievable. Sixty-one thousand people created Facebook fundraisers thanks to the ACS Relay for Life Challenge on Facebook. After the event was completed, ACS reaped over four hundred thousand new donor leads. These leads also represented a huge return on investment with an average cost per lead of only $3.12. And it was even cost-efficient to get people involved in the challenge in the first place. For some perspective, the industry benchmark to acquire a peer-to-peer fundraiser registrant for a social fundraiser is $600 per individual. For the ACS 2020 Challenge on Facebook, the cost was only $22.41. Amidst all this energy, the ACS Fundraiser Challenge on Facebook broke the fundraising record for Facebook when, in October 2020, they received over 23,000 donations in a single day, totaling over a million dollars.

With all this success, however, ACS wanted to know that their current work in the digital space would not eclipse their decades of experience in Relay for Life. What we discovered, however, was that 95 percent of ACS Challenge participants were new to the organization. This meant that Challenges on Facebook provided all the engagement that an in-person event might have without sucking away any financial support from their in-person campaigns. After the challenge month was over, the national vice president for Relay for Life commented that "[ACS] exceeded every goal with this pilot. It won't replace our traditional peer-to-peer fundraising, but it will work alongside it to bring in new constituents and drive revenue."

Making Facebook Challenges a Part of Your Fundraising Strategy

Facebook Challenges are an essential part of your social fundraising strategy. Those who don't invest in these powerful digital events risk leaving valuable support on the table. And with new generations of digital natives growing into the world of philanthropy, having a strong social fundraising strategy will be essential to continued success for your nonprofit. As social fundraising expands into new platforms, understanding how you create these campaigns on Facebook will inform your tactics in other social channels. In order to create a compelling Facebook Challenge, you first need to *establish the parameters of your Challenge.*

Your Challenge parameters describe the foundational aspects of your fundraiser. Think of it like the road map that guides both your fundraising team and your social supporters throughout the Challenge. Best practices for setting these parameters include:

Duration—How long is your Facebook Challenge? It can be anywhere from one day to a month or more. In setting up the duration of your Facebook Challenge, consider the supporters you're trying to reach. Are these digital natives tied to their social feeds who could raise thousands in a day? Or are your supporters spending less time on socials?

Activity—What are your supporters doing? In the ACS example, we provided supporters various physical activities such as walking a set number of steps, but the activity should inspire action in your supporters. Maybe your supporter base prefers to read books than exercise. You can set a Challenge activity based around reading a number of books per month while they raise funds for your organization.

Goals—What do you want your supporters to achieve? Setting goals for your Facebook Challenge will provide you a benchmark on your campaign's progress. Consider how much you want to raise overall and how much you want your social supporters to raise. Set a participation goal, as well, to include how many registrants you aim to have joined the challenge and the corresponding Facebook Group. This will give you a clear picture of any conversion problems you may run into.

The parameters give you boundaries for your Facebook Challenge and help you get a clear picture of the overall scope of the campaign. Once you've created these, take time to think about the participants that will sign up for your Challenge. How they engage with your Facebook Challenge will dictate how successful your efforts will be. Craft an exciting participant experience that makes your supporters feel like their contribution has an impact on your cause. Here are some questions to consider in regard to the Challenge participant experience:

- *How are they raising funds?* Share with them the standard goal for a fundraiser but give them the ability to raise whatever they feel they can accomplish. Provide them with best practices around fundraising through Messenger so they can achieve their goals.

- *What is their progress in the Challenge activity?* Encourage them to keep up with their activity goals through Messenger and to track their progress in and outside of the group. This opens up your brand to new audiences and creates new connections between participants.

- *What is their role in the Challenge group?* Set them up for success in the group by outlining the purpose of the group, how they can use it, and any admin guidelines for safe conversations.

This last part, the dynamics of the Challenge group, is perhaps one of the most important aspects of Challenges on Facebook. To make this group feel like a community, prompt the participants to share their experiences and stories through discussion starters. These could be posts asking for folks to provide updates on their challenge or fundraising activities. You could use the Challenge group to provide them with tips and encouragement throughout the period. This is your time to talk to the participants directly. To reach them authentically, make sure you're relying on your nonprofit's brand guidelines when you communicate through the Challenge group.

Now that you've done the groundwork for your Facebook Challenge, it's time to find your participants. Using Facebook Ads allows you to attract participants who are already in-channel and engaging with their Facebook feed. These are exactly the kinds of new supporters you want. By creating a targeted ad campaign, users can find your Challenge on their feed where, within a few clicks, they can sign up for the Challenge and join the group. When creating your ads, target both audiences that are familiar to you and those that you might not know. Try to target an audience of members that are most like your supporters on Facebook. Or you might go after users who like a page that has similar values to yours. This increases your reach into new audiences to become new supporters of your cause.

Challenges are a great way to raise funds and empower a set of supporters. With these new supporters, the challenge for the nonprofit is how to retain their attention and action after the event is over. Many nonprofits think they can just add these new supporters to their email subscription list and that will somehow turn into donations. These new leads, however, have already shown you that they want to engage through social channels. So to keep the momentum of this flywheel going, you've got to establish a connection with these people. And there's already a tool built into Facebook for you to start a direct conversation with them—Facebook Messenger.

Nick's Tips

- Facebook Challenges require a set of parameters including duration, participant activity, and fundraising goals that give both the nonprofit and the fundraiser goal posts throughout the campaign.

- Nonprofits can use Facebook Challenge groups to create a community where the participants can connect with the organization and each other.

- To expand into new audiences, use Facebook Ads to bring in supporters who may be unfamiliar with your organization.

- In order to continue the momentum of these events, engage with participants in-channel to keep them invested in your organization's cause.

CHAPTER FIVE

Starting the Conversation

There's an old adage that we have two ears and one mouth so that we can listen twice as well as we speak. And still so few take the time to hear out those around them. We all have our stories we want to tell, but it's rare that someone is available to listen. When we can spare a moment, we reserve our listening skills for those we find are most important. In the nonprofit space, this tendency is most prominent when an organization listens to the needs and desires of their highest ticket donors—the ones they deem "important." They exhaust considerable effort to reach these wealthy supporters. But when it comes to engaging with their remaining donor population, they are out of resources. Through big galas and charity drives, they act like they're listening to their donors, but in reality, these events leave a majority of their supporters unheard.

We know that this isn't always for lack of trying. We've mentioned several times that the prevailing belief among nonprofits is that it is too difficult to take the time to hear out every single one of their donors. There are just too many of them! It's definitely easier to send out an email to your donor list and call it a day. But the needs of the average nonprofit donor are changing. Donors want to hear from the organizations who are on the front lines fighting for the causes they care about. They want to know their money has an impact. They want to be a part of the conversation of your organization and help you accomplish your mission. Thankfully, social media—and chatbots—have made it easier than ever to listen to your donors.

Let's face it: we hate chatbots. They seem impersonal and inauthentic. They suck the humanity out of the digital space and make us feel lied to. For brands, they're often deployed to efficiently handle inquiries and make sure that person gets the right information or talks to the right person. Artificial Intelligence technology is evolving (and there are ways it can help your nonprofit) but the average chatbot isn't empowered with the latest ChatGPT technology. They're not meant to provide information or be a valuable source of support. And we get frustrated when they can't understand what we're saying or meeting our needs in the way a human would. For all of this, however, they can provide one thing that humans often fail at—a listening ear.

We have already talked about how you can support fundraisers led by your community of donors through the various tools provided through social media platforms. When that fundraiser comes to an end, however, what happens to your supporters? You know they're dedicated to your cause, but have you considered how they want to be involved in your organization? In that first instance of fundraising, be it through a Challenge or on their own, it's like your donors have gone on a first date with your nonprofit. They're excited and passionate about your cause, and maybe still a little amped up from that fundraiser. They made the first move by fundraising for you. Now, they're looking to you for the next step in this relationship.

Conversational messaging, using social messengers to connect with your donor base in an authentic way, is the way to build this one-on-one relationship with everyone in your donor base. Through Facebook Messenger, you can start deeper conversations with your donor base to understand why they support your cause, create opportunities for them to get involved, and build unique relationships with each donor. This works especially well for social fundraisers that have already engaged with your organization on social media. According to our research at GoodUnited, we've found that in-channel messaging through Facebook is fifty-four times more effective than email in getting those social fundraisers to take action. Additionally, those engaged through conversational messaging are 20 percent more likely to raise funds for your cause a second time.

This gets us back to the topic of chatbots. When deployed with conversational messaging, these automatons are the perfect way to gather insights about your donors and create repeatable action. Like I mentioned earlier, chatbots are really good at one thing—providing a listening space for the human user. Used effectively, however, they're able to do more than that. By empowering your Messenger bot with conversational messaging tactics, your supporters are more likely to engage with the bot. This lays the foundation for further conversations and a real relationship with this donor. Consider these tips as you're building out your conversational messaging strategies on social media.

Express Gratitude. One of the simplest ways to get donors invested in your organization is to thank them for what they have done for you. Whether it was for participating in a Challenge or raising funds on their own, they'll appreciate the thanks. It shows that you've been paying attention to their donation and that it has had a real impact on the cause. You can always provide status updates on your organization's fight with the cause in your gratitude. That will tie the donor's work directly back to your cause. You can also be simple and provide a "Thank you for your donation." This gratitude, however, is meant to be a conversation starter. It's meant to open a door to your donor, so be ready to take the next step.

Understand Why. Use social messaging to get a good idea of why they gave to your cause and what led them to your organization. How are they affected by your cause? Are they impacted directly or is it a friend or family member? The information you're gathering here will be useful data in further fundraising endeavors. It can, however, become a complicated conversation with a lot of input from your donor. Now multiply that by all your donors and you can see how the data you're getting from these conversations can become massive and complicated. Thankfully, there are ways to streamline the conversation experience so you're getting the data you need. At Stop Soldier Suicide, for example, they provide easy click-through responses that guide the user's conversation so that they get accurate and useful information.

Assist Their Support of Your Cause. Once you understand why they support your cause, find out how to get them involved further. If they gave as part of a Facebook fundraising challenge, ask them if they'd like to be a part of future Challenges relevant to their interest. If they participated in a 5K, for instance, offer them another physical challenge. On the other hand, maybe they can't participate in a challenge, but they want to volunteer. Give them volunteering opportunities within your organization that keep them engaged with your nonprofit. As you're building your conversational messaging, consider these various paths your donors might choose and how you provide them with ways to grow closer to your organization.

Finally, *Speak Authentically.* As we know, the social fundraiser is digitally savvy. They navigate ads and bots every day. They know how to choose wisely when they engage with an organization. To cut through the noise, your Messenger tactics must seem authentic to both your organization and to the fundraiser. If you've maintained a Facebook Challenge group, you'll know this is vital to any communication you have with your donors. Again, rely on the branded language that you've already established for your nonprofit to maximize success.

Chatting with Best Friends Animal Society

To see the power of conversational messaging in action, let's return to Best Friends Animal Society, one of GoodUnited's early adopters. This nonprofit was mentioned earlier when I told the story of the elderly supporter who named Best Friends in her will. This animal welfare nonprofit was founded in 1984 with a mission to help end kill shelters in America by 2025. Before we started working with them, their primary fundraiser to accomplish this goal was Strut Your Mutt, a national fundraiser pet walk with hubs across the country. In 2019, this in-person event raised over $2.7 million to advance their no-kill mission. Just like Relay for Life and the American Cancer Society, Strut Your Mutt was integral to Best Friend's continued mission.

Then in 2020, they realized, much like every other nonprofit, they needed to pivot to maintain their fundraising stream. They had established and maintained some social media strategy, but it was more focused on providing information and updates through their social channels. When they approached us, they wanted to better understand how peer-to-peer social fundraising could expand their brand into new audiences. They wanted to reach younger folks as well as people outside of their selected regions. Additionally, they wished to engage their strong network of supporters with a new digital-first event to supplement their lost income from the canceled Strut Your Mutt campaign. Unfortunately, like many nonprofits, Best Friends didn't have the resources to create and realize their social giving strategy on their own.

In their partnership with GoodUnited, Best Friends were able to engage their legacy supporters and seek out new donor bases. In concert with their team, GoodUnited created targeted ads to go after new audiences, segmented out donors, crafted message copy, and moderated their challenge groups. Unsurprisingly, we found that a majority of their supporters were familiar with Best Friends through the Strut Your Mutt event. Due to this, we partnered with the organization to create a thirty-mile Facebook Challenge as a virtual alternative to their in-person walk event. The overall low-cost point of this event took the pressure off those at Best Friends. This challenge event allowed the organization to focus their efforts on other fundraising streams and push forward their mission. It was also crucial in recouping costs lost due to the COVID pandemic.

Within the Facebook Challenge group, conversations among the participants were always bubbling up. At the heights of COVID, these pet owners were missing the connection that they had once gotten at dog parks, or out on group walks, which is why when the topic "How Have Your Pets Saved You?" was first posted by the Best Friends moderator, everyone in the group had something to say. Group members shared how their pets helped them through COVID, or other difficult moments in their lives. Through these stories, members connected to each other and to the Best Friends organization. In-app messaging supported these connections by reminding them about their challenge and offering other resources provided by the Best Friends organization.

In the Facebook Challenge alone, Best Friends raised over $100,000 for their no-kill mission—a near 400 percent return on their initial investment. A majority of these donations came from donors brand-new to their organization. Eighty-five percent of the email addresses gained through the Facebook Challenge were new to the Best Friends marketing database. In this case, they also accomplished their goal to reach new audiences. Working with Best Friends, GoodUnited offered a strategy that had a lower buy-in cost for a huge return—the potential for a whole new generation of donors. Through email and in-app messaging, Best Friends targeted their new leads to offer them opportunities to support their mission of ending kill shelters in America.

These newcomers to Best Friends represented a huge potential for the organization if they engaged them correctly using conversational messaging. After the challenge, participants were offered the chance to opt-in to updates through Messenger from Best Friends. Leveraging conversational messaging strategies, they started chatting with these donors to gauge their engagement and provide them with volunteering and fundraising opportunities. As they began to have these conversations with their donors, Best Friends realized the impact the Challenge experience had on their fundraisers. And as you may remember, they built the kind of relationships with their donors that caused one of them to name them a beneficiary in their will.

Building one-on-one relationships with your supporters *is* possible through conversational messaging and the opportunities it provides. Through Messenger, you're able to open up a window directly to your supporters and start conversations with them. You can thank them for their support and encourage them to continue.

By asking the right questions, you learn how they're connected to your cause. You understand these supporters' motivations and interests allowing you to tailor your responses to best engage with them. And the best part? It's cost-effective. Conversational messaging through social media makes it so that you can make moves with every single one of your supporters for the fraction of the cost of an influential in-person event.

Cultivating Affinity in Your Base

You don't need to land a beneficiary, as Best Friends Animal Society did, to harness the potential of conversational messaging. By reaching out to your supporters via social messaging throughout the year, your nonprofit builds on your relationships with those donors. Consider: you lead a cancer nonprofit dedicated to finding a cure to the disease. Your organization hosts a Facebook Challenge where one of the participants reveals they recently received a cancer diagnosis. You learned this information from ongoing social messenger updates. As a part of your organization, you have resources for cancer patients who are just beginning the treatment. So, through Messenger, you provide links to these resources to the donor. By monitoring this person's responses and providing resources from your organization, you can check in with them at regular intervals to continue building affinity with this supporter.

And, thanks to the immediacy of Facebook Messenger, you're able to do this at scale with your entire donor base. Think of the best relationships you've had—friendships, partners, or family members. Do you just communicate with them once a year? If you're on good terms with them, probably not. You're probably chatting with them on a regular basis that makes sense for your relationship. It should be the same for your donors. To build affinity with your donor base, you must communicate with them in the cadence and style that appeals best to them.

This all comes down to how they see themselves as part of your organization. Do they just want to raise funds for you on their birthday? Great! Every year a week before their birthday, thank them for fundraising for them in years past, and remind them how to start their Facebook birthday fundraiser for this year. Do they want to volunteer every week? Super! Connect them to a volunteer coordinator who can provide them weekly volunteering opportunities. Do they only want to participate in Facebook Challenges? Amazing! Give them information on the upcoming Challenge in your fundraising calendar. No matter how they want to be involved, accept it and make it happen for them.

As you build these relationships, you will gain more and more data on your supporters that allow you to take action. If their experience of your organization is good, you can rely on their continued support. As years go by, their support may fluctuate or change depending on various factors out of your control. If you've engaged them on their terms, however, you may get a donor who returns down the road or perhaps even wants to name your organization as a beneficiary. Building affinity means you've spent the time to listen to your donors and provide them a space within your organization. And it all starts with the low investment of sending them a few Facebook messages. So, open up that chat window and get to typing. Your supporters are waiting for you.

Nick's Tips

- Conversational messaging is when you use social messengers to connect with your donor base in an authentic way. It's the way to build this one-on-one relationship with every supporter of your cause.

- When creating conversational messaging tactics, speak to your supporters in an authentic way that reflects your nonprofit's brand and voice.

- Use Messenger to express gratitude to your supporters to start a deeper conversation about their support.

- Understand your supporters by asking why they engage with your nonprofit and how they'd like to be more involved.

- Provide them ways to become a part of your nonprofit's cause through volunteer opportunities and future fundraising efforts.

- Build on this relationship throughout the year to create a deeper and more long-term connection with these supporters.

CHAPTER SIX

The Trends in Giving

Maintaining regular contact throughout the year with your supporters builds affinity between them and your nonprofit. A lot can happen, however, during those 365 days. As the days roll by, supporter behaviors can fluctuate based on a variety of factors—some of which you can't predict. Natural disasters, national tragedies, and other news items can influence how much your donors are able to give and where your supporters are focusing their efforts. On the other hand, there are also huge generational trends that, while easier to spot, have a significant impact on your nonprofit's fundraising stream. Understanding how your base's behavior fluctuates both throughout the year and throughout the lifetime of your organization is key to future-proofing your fundraising efforts.

To understand this, you only need to look at the "shopping holidays" of the last week of November to see how donor behavior and consumer behavior overlap. First, we shop for Black Friday deals. The next day we support our local businesses with Small Business Saturday. After that comes Cyber Monday for buying the things we can only find online. Once all of the shopping is done, we donate to our favorite causes on Giving Tuesday. For Americans, the week after Thanksgiving boasts some of the highest per capita spending on both consumer goods and nonprofit donations. In 2021 alone, retailers raked in over $13.4 billion on Black Friday.[13] A few days later, the Giving Tuesday Data Commons reported $2.7 billion raised for nonprofits across the country.[14] Both nonprofit and for-profit organizations can see this spike in their efforts as the year comes to an end and the weather turns cold. They expect this seasonal bump to meet their important year-end deadlines.

I have an open secret for you: what you call donors, for-profit companies call customers. These companies spend billions every year to understand the life cycle of their customers to maximize their profits. They want to know everything they can about a customer's behavior. And some nonprofits do this as well. As they come to understand their donor base, they see how their support ebbs and flows in their fundraising efforts over time. When you understand these fluctuations, you can create better fundraising strategies that garner the most donations for your organization. These changes, however, represent more than just annual holiday spending. Generational transitions, national news cycles, and even personal milestones can impact how your organization raises funds.

In previous chapters, we've explored who your donors are and how they give. We've seen how, through a frictionless one-click to

---

13   Jonathan Greig, "Black Friday spending in the US falls to $8.9 billion as shoppers start earlier in November," ZDNet, November 29, 2021, https://www.zdnet.com/article/black-friday-spending-in-us-falls-to-8-9-billion-adobe/.

14   GivingTuesday, "Millions of people come together to celebrate generosity, share kindness, and drive ecord-breaking giving on GivingTuesday 2021," GivingTuesday Data Commons, December 1, 2021, givingtuesday.org/blog/millions-of-people-come-together-to-celebrate-generosity-share-kindness-and-drive-record-breaking-giving-on-givingtuesday-2021/.

give process, we make the donation process easier than it's ever been before. Through using Facebook Messenger, you start to learn about your donor's passions, motivations, and support for your cause. In these conversations, you build one-on-one relationships with your donors based on a clear understanding of what drives them. Your donors, however, are not static points that patiently wait by their Facebook app for a message from you. They are dynamic human beings with their own lived experiences that may not revolve around your nonprofit. To best serve them, you must consider how they change and grow as your nonprofit does.

Even if a nonprofit is using legacy fundraising techniques, they're still tracking donor behavior over time. Data points like recency, frequency, and value of their donations help their fundraising wing understand how to engage with individual donors. It's how they decide who gets an invitation to the gala that year and who doesn't. Despite this tracking, there is a sea change on the horizon that will have massive implications for nonprofits across the country. The wealth in this country is about to change hands from one generation to another. This change will impact how you manage your fundraising efforts, and it's as inevitable as time itself.

Currently, you probably already know that Baby Boomers (the generation born between 1946 and 1964) make up a large portion of your donor population. This generation accounts for 43 percent of all charitable donations in the United States each year.[15] The reason? Boomers control a considerable amount of the wealth in this country. To capture that wealth, the giving experience has historically been tailored to fit boomer expectations. Throughout the years, nonprofit

---

15   Nhu Te, "Generational trends: donors are researching nonprofits before they give," *NonProfit Pro*, March 11, 2020, https://www.nonprofitpro.com/article/generational-trends-donors-are-researching-nonprofits-before-they-give.

and for-profit organizations have come to understand that the Boomer generation are largely brand loyal. They tend to give over and over again to organizations without a deep consideration of the cause.

This is one reason in-person events are the most popular fundraising tool for nonprofits—they're popular with Boomers. These kinds of events have strong branding that resonates with this generation. From t-shirts to water bottles, the branded materials offered help Baby Boomers feel a part of an organization in a way that meets their expectations. And, until 2020, these tactics were wildly successful. Many nonprofits are perfectly happy to reap the massive benefits of these in-person events. If it's not broken, they think, why fix them? What they fail to realize is that the giving power of this generation is about to change hands to their successors, and it's happening faster than they might expect.

The issue with making a big bet on generational trends is that one day that generation's influence will wane and the power they once wielded will transfer to the next. We're seeing that play out today in our country. By 2045, in fact, Generation X and the millennial generation will inherit over $84 trillion from their boomer parents.[16] This transition means that a new population of individuals with new needs and desires are about to have more buying power than they did before. Many for-profit companies have already experienced this transition and are pivoting their own messaging to appeal to these populations. Yet nonprofits continue to lag behind and focus on tactics that are quickly going out of style.

To attract this new generation of givers, we must understand how they view philanthropy differently than previous generations. One

---

16   Cerulli Associates, "Cerulli anticipates $84 trillion in wealth transfers through 2045," Cerulli Associates press release, January 20, 2022, https://www.cerulli.com/press-releases/cerulli-anticipates-84-trillion-in-wealth-transfers-through-2045.

initial difference is that Millennials and Gen-Xers are much more likely to be cause-focused than brand-focused. Whether it be access to healthcare or climate change, these generations adopt causes as their own and allow those causes to guide them. In every purchase they make, every organization they support, and every choice they make, they seek to be as socially conscious as possible.[17] Seventy percent of Millennials say they prefer to work at an organization that engages in some form of corporate social responsibility and 47 percent cite that social responsibility influences their buying habits.[18] Unlike Baby Boomers, who are brand loyal to a nonprofit, these next generations of givers want to know that the decisions they make influence the overall social good.

Social responsibility is key to these younger generations of givers. They expect the organizations they support to have an impact on the causes that are important to them. This means they are more interested in a specific cause than any particular nonprofit. Unlike their parents, Millennials and Gen-Xers are brand agnostic: they just want to ensure the nonprofit is making strides in the cause they support. A donor from a younger generation that wants to join the fight against breast cancer, for example, will give to the organization that has demonstrated the biggest impact in that cause. Boomers, on the other hand, are more likely to give to an organization that they (or their friends) have given to before. They are less concerned with the impact of their donation. Demonstrating their social responsibility, however, is very important to Millennials. They make sure everyone knows they

---

17   Richard H. Levey, "Millennials value everyday social good above cash donations," Nonprofit Times, May 6, 2021, https://www.thenonprofittimes.com/report/millennials-value-everyday-social-good-above-cash-donations/.

18   Fidelity Charitable, "The future of philanthropy," January 2021, https://www.fidelitycharitable.org/insights/2021-future-of-philanthropy.html.

support a cause by advocating for it on their social platforms to their friends and followers.

Which leads us to the next difference in these new generations: they grew up on social platforms. They value authenticity in their experiences with social media. Due to this, they're more likely to trust their inner circle of friends than any organization. They're able to deftly navigate these digital spaces. They use these platforms to tell their own stories and connect with their friends. It's these stories and connections that influence the giving behavior of their followers. While these donors appreciate the frictionless social giving experience, it goes deeper than that. Right after they hit that "donate now" button, they're able to share their experiences with the nonprofit and why they are a part of this cause. Now, when their followers see their friend's story about why they gave to a cause, they're more likely to give to that same organization that's been verified by their social network.

So, what does this mean for the expansion that social giving represents? First off, if you're relying on legacy in-person events for the majority of your fundraising activities, you may still be reaping the benefits of the Boomer generation. You may soon regret that, however, when that steady fundraising stream from in-person events turns to a trickle. To best prepare for this change, adopt social giving strategies to work in tandem with your established fundraising tactics. Second, digital natives like Millennials and generations beyond can easily sniff out inauthenticity in a brand. If you're trying to sell them on a mission without the credibility to back it up, they just won't support you. Nor will you get access to their larger social networks. When messaging to these populations, ensure that you've got the evidence to prove you've done the work. With wealth eventually transferring to new generations, your organization can't afford to ignore the preferences of these emerging donors.

The power of social giving allows you to have a one-on-one relationship with each of your donors. It's these authentic relationships that bring your millennial donors into your organization where they can feel like they are pushing your cause forward. Through Messenger, you can learn more about them and show them real stories of impact thanks to their donation. With Challenges, you grow on those relationships and create communities among like-minded supporters. And with continual check-ins, you are able to address the concerns and needs of your donors as they grow with your organization. By building on this relationship, you create a donor base that doesn't only give once or twice a year, but continually supports your cause throughout their lifetimes—until Generation Z takes the wheel.

> **With wealth eventually transferring to new generations, your organization can't afford to ignore the preferences of these emerging donors.**

The News Cycle and Giving

Generational trends in giving can be easy to prepare for if you can read between the donation lines. They have longer cycles, leaving you time to prepare your organization for the needs of a new donor base. If we think about these trends like the tide, the fluctuations between generations are large waves you can see coming from the horizon. Yet there are more sudden storms of giving that can surprise the nonprofit. Some nonprofits have had to contend with sudden deluges of donations whipped up by our twenty-four-seven news cycle. And with the explosive growth of social giving, breaking news stories can flood your organization with new donors from unexpected places.

Stories wash over us every day. From our commutes filled with talk radio, catching the news on the television in a waiting room, or just the idle moments where we stare at our social media feed, we consume more media on average than we ever have before. In 2020, media consumption spiked up 3.1 percent—an increase not seen in over fifteen years.[19] This surge is partly thanks to the COVID pandemic where lockdown placed us all permanently on the couch. But another driving force is the proliferation of digital media platforms for breaking news. According to research from Pew, eight in ten Americans get their news from their smartphone or tablet device. In addition, 53 percent say they get a majority of their news from their social media feed.[20] How we consume news media has shaped the way we view and act upon our world.

And, as we know, social media has provided a space for people to tell their own stories. Your perspective can now join the current of a breaking news headline by tapping that share button. You can add your own take on your social feed where your friends can share, like, or comment themselves. As these streams cross, high-visibility viral stories can strike at the heart of a social media user, driving them to take action. For example, you see an article from a local news publication on your feed about a young boy who requires medical attention

---

19   Nina Lentini, "Expect jagged growth of media consumption as saturation point nears," Marketing Dive, January 13, 2022, https://www.marketingdive.com/news/expect-jagged-growth-of-media-consumption-as-saturation-point-nears.

20   Elisa Shearer, "More than eight-in-ten Americans get news from digital devices," Pew Research Center, January 12, 2021, https://www.pewresearch.org/fact-tank/2021/01/12/more-than-eight-in-ten-americans-get-news-from-digital-devices/.

after a tragic accident. At the end of the article, there's a link to the family's social fundraising page. You might donate $20 for yourself. But then, because you really want to help this family, you might take the extra step to share their story on your feed. More people see the article, more donations come in, and the family meets their goal.

These viral stories can also attract the nation's attention. Huge news stories can result in a downpour of donations for nonprofits whose cause is grabbing headlines. But the news cycle is as unpredictable as the weather. A cause becomes trendy and garners thousands of donations one week, only to endure a dry spell that lasts for months after their short time in the spotlight. After the death of George Floyd in 2020, for example, the Black Lives Matter Global foundation took in over $90 million in donations, quickly making them one of the most influential groups fighting for racial equality.[21]

Some organizations even plan for these rapid infusions of donations and only raise funds necessary to fight sudden disasters. "Gray Sky nonprofits" like the Red Cross and Team Rubicon only actively fundraise in the midst of natural disasters like hurricanes and earthquakes. Just as we learned in previous chapters, no matter when people are in need, there are usually others who are willing to help. Fueled by dedicated reporting on national issues, we are confronted by stories of people contending with tragedies on a daily basis. People see images of their fellow humans in need every day on their social feeds, and it compels them to give.

What happens in our world and how it is reflected on our social media feed influences the organizations we give to and the causes we support. The sudden impulse to give has been called "rage-

---

21 Aaron Morrison, "Exclusive: Black lives matter opens up about its finances," Los Angeles Times, February 23, 2021, https://www.latimes.com/world-nation/ story/2021-02-23/ap-exclusive-black-lives-matter-opens-up-about-its-finances.

giving," due to the anger some people feel about specific headlines and their tendency to smash the donate button to make their voice heard. National figures can also drive our giving behavior. There is a shorthand phrase that some nonprofits use that encapsulates this phenomenon—the Trump Bump. Regardless of how you feel about the forty-fifth president of the United States, Donald Trump mentioning a cause or a nonprofit's name can result in massive donations from both sides of the aisle. In the early days of his presidency, the website ragedonate.com—which is no longer in service—would take his direct quotes and use them to bolster fundraising campaigns for many left-leaning organizations.[22] These Trump Bumps, while tempestuous, brought in a lot of donations for organizations that may not have been used to the national spotlight.

When it comes to giving based on news stories, social giving has continued to prove valuable to organizations and social fundraisers alike. In June 2018, The Refugee and Immigration Center for Legal Services, or RAICES, became the center of a nation-wide storm that had been raging around immigration on our southern border. It started with a photo of a young girl in a pink shirt, her face streaked with tears. Illuminated by a stark white flashlight, she stares up at the legs of two immigration officers who are arresting her mother. This photo, taken by John Moore from Getty Images, was used under a headline in the *New York Times* about children being separated from their parents at the border.[23] After that article was posted, the photo went viral and became a powerful symbol for people who sought to

---

22   Michael Conklin, "Was the 'Trump bump' a one-time phenomenon for charities?" November 5, 2019. 32 CHRON. PHILANTHROPY 50, https://ssrn.com/abstract=3608736.

23   Julie Hirschfeld Davis and Michael D. Shear, "How Trump came to enforce a practice of separating migrant families," New York Times, June 16, 2018, https://www.nytimes.com/2018/06/16/us/politics/family-separation-trump.html.

reunite these children with their parents. People like Charlotte and David Wilner who saw the photo were inspired to create a Facebook fundraiser entitled "Reunite an immigrant parent with their child."

The Wilners chose to fundraise for RAICES on Facebook, a company for which they both formerly worked. They were infuriated by what they had seen in the media regarding migrant families, and that image in particular motivated them to take action. Parents of toddlers themselves, the prospect of a young girl being taken away from her parents horrified them. In a later interview conducted by the *New York Times*, Charlotte Wilner declared that it was the only way she felt she could bring any comfort to that girl. It was a Saturday when they created the Facebook fundraiser with a modest goal of raising $1,500. Right above their goal, the picture of the crying girl in pink was the banner for the page.

Six days later, they met their goal and then some, raising over $20 million for RAICES. Over 525,000 Facebook users logged on to contribute to the Wilners' page. One Tuesday afternoon, the page was bringing in over $3,000 a minute. The fundraising page became a bit of a philanthropic storm surge for RAICES, who were stunned, delighted, and a bit anxious to receive these donations. When asked for comment by the *New York Times*, the executive director of RAICES admitted that "those moments of joy [for the success of the fundraiser] are curtailed by a realization of great responsibility."[24]

Moments of heavy donations like this can happen to any organization. Yet to simply call these instances *rage*-giving doesn't feel accurate. Humans are motivated to give by a multitude of factors that can change in an instant. We sometimes give out of righteous anger

---

24 Julia Jacobs, "They wanted to raise $1,500 for immigrant families at the border. They got over $20 million," New York Times, June 19, 2018, https://www.nytimes.com/2018/06/19/us/raices-charity-border-immigrants.html.

to feel useful in an endless news cycle. But other times, we give out of joy either at a holiday or a special occasion. We also give when we're saddened by a tragedy that feels out of our control. Ultimately, our various impulses to give are unique to who we are and how we view the world. How then can an organization prepare for something that is out of their control? Here are some things to look out for when news trends intersect with your fundraising efforts.

First off, *understand your organization's story and the stories about your cause.* This is your first step as being seen as authentic and impactful in the eyes of your donor base. If you're a nonprofit organized to help hungry children, news items about school lunch debt might be more important to your cause than ones about healthcare costs. As you're staying on top of the news related to your cause, consider how you're speaking about your mission through your fundraising efforts. When news items related to your cause do take off, you'll want to have a deep understanding of what the news story is and how it specifically intersects with your organization. You'll want to demonstrate your history of supporting the cause and how you've been relevant to the conversation before the media was paying attention.

As you're doing this, *know the stories that your donors and supporters care about.* If you've been using Messenger to communicate with them, you should have a good understanding of what kind of news they're interested in and what topics they follow. We've spoken a lot about bad news in this chapter, but great stories about impact around a cause also get picked up by the media. Think about how you can highlight stories related to your cause for your donor base to demonstrate impact. This continues to bring them into the organization they support and makes them a part of your cause's story.

Finally, *identify organizations whose causes are in alignment with yours.* By partnering with these kinds of organizations, you can broaden your organization's reach and highlight your dedication to fighting your cause. Say, for instance, you're a nonprofit based out of Des Moines advocating for public housing and efforts to support the homeless population. While you may be working to help those in Des Moines, research the organizations in other cities who share in your mission. What national-level issues unite your two organizations, and how can you join forces to influence change in both cities? By partnering with other organizations, you not only forward your own nonprofit, but you're also able to push your cause forward in a substantial way.

> Social giving represents a new way to quickly respond to volatile times as well as prepare for new waves of supporters for your cause.

Fluctuations within your supporter base are expected. Whether it be big generational changes or sudden news-related spikes, it's important to prepare your nonprofit's fundraising stream for uncertainty. Social giving represents a new way to quickly respond to volatile times as well as prepare for new waves of supporters for your cause. By leveraging the best practices we've outlined in social giving, you'll gain invaluable data that will allow you to take action even in the most uncertain times. Don't wait for a rainy day to implement them.

Nick's Tips

- Supporter behavior fluctuates over time—whether those be generational trends that impact fundraising methods or breaking news stories that intersect with your organization's cause.

- New generations are influencing the world of philanthropy. They are more socially conscious and demand an authentic connection to the causes they support. To best engage them, learn their motivations through Messenger, and deliver stories of impact to demonstrate your work in the cause.

- The news cycle can influence who gives to your organization and why. To take advantage of these sudden spikes in giving, ensure you are engaging with news stories that impact your cause. To best reach new supporters, demonstrate your history of supporting the newsworthy cause before it was a media sensation.

- Consider partnering with organizations across the country to expand your organization's reach and drive real change in your cause.

CHAPTER SEVEN

Surfing Other Platforms of Social Giving

In 2021, TikTok, a popular video social media platform, introduced Garden for Good, a game for users of their app. The game was a farming simulator where players could grow digital crops that mature in minutes, not months. If you once had a farm on Facebook's Farmville, you've tilled virtual fields like these before. TikTok users could access their gardens through a widget on their For You Page (FYP), which is not dissimilar to a Facebook feed. It's a curated feed of videos that are relevant to a user's interests and the interests of their followers. TikTok users spend a majority of their time on their FYP and use it to post videos, stitch to other videos, and generally share content. What they don't often find on this page are farming simulator games.

That's why, when Garden for Good launched, it represented a different tactic for the video platform—and a head-scratching one at that. Garden for Good was one of TikTok's first forays into the world of social giving. In this game, users could cultivate crops to exchange for real monetary donations from TikTok to Feeding America. For every digital bundle of corn, cabbage, or wheat harvested, TikTok would donate anywhere between fifty cents and two dollars to the nonprofit. Despite Garden of Good's different use case, the app was popular with a few TikTok users. They grew and donated as many crops as they wanted so contributions were only limited by the amount of people playing the game. And yet, it never went truly viral. By December 2021, the simulator had been removed from the app.

In the past chapters, we have shown you how social giving is the new mode of philanthropy that expands donor pools, creates frictionless giving experiences, and builds a community of support-ers for your cause. In every instance, however, we've only covered case studies from Facebook and their giving tools. But even the most unplugged person knows that people aren't *just* on Facebook. According to the Digital 2022 Global Overview report created in collaboration with HootSuite, there are currently 4.62 billion social media users across the globe. The report goes further to say that these users, on average, engage with at least seven social platforms on a daily basis.[25]

Despite all this, Facebook still reigns large in social platforms and represents the leaders in this next wave of social giving. As of the publication of this book, Facebook stands heads and shoulders above other platforms with 2.9 billion users. It's not just the wealth of users, however, that makes Facebook the standout platform

---

25   Simon Kemp, "Digital 2022: Global overview report," January 26, 2022, https://datareportal.com/reports/digital-2022-global-overview-report.

for social giving. They've raised over $7 billion for worthy causes around the world since they first rolled out their social giving tools in 2015. And a big reason they've raised so much comes down to the fact that they've just been in the social giving game longer. They have almost a decade's worth of experience when it comes to social giving.

All of this experience means that Facebook's giving capabilities are simply more mature and have found fit with their users. It's the only platform that provides tools and communities that nonprofits can use today to maximize their revenue. With an eye on this success, however, other social platforms have begun testing out their own giving tools. Some have had success, while others have had rocky starts. While TikTok's Garden for Good enabled users to fundraise on their app, the game was counterintuitive to the natural use case of the app. In other words, people use TikTok to watch and make video content, and not to play farming simulators. Today, however, they've learned their lesson and are experimenting with new methods that we will get into a bit later.

Instagram, LinkedIn, YouTube, and Twitch are also directing resources toward researching and developing social giving tools that are unique to their platforms and their users. While all of these solutions are at different stages of development, these companies see the value in social giving and want to be a part of this expansion in philanthropy. To better understand how these other platforms can be beneficial to you and your social giving strategy, let's take a look at these platforms outside of Facebook, and how their giving tools currently function. In this chapter, we'll show you how you can leverage the new populations on these platforms, understand how users engage with the platform, and how you can shift your messaging to appeal to these new audiences.

There is one thing to consider before you read too far into these other platforms. Know that, if you've implemented the social giving strategies we've already outlined in this book, your social giving strategy is *already* well on its way to success. The messaging that you use to connect with your donor base on Facebook will serve you as you take on new social platforms. Your keen knowledge of your Facebook followers will lead you to research the users on these other platforms and let that research guide your decisions. When choosing to expand to other platforms, it's best for you to do all the analysis you did for your social strategy on Facebook before you move into these other platforms for social giving. It's up to you to decide whether or not it is worth the effort. With that, let's find out!

> When choosing to expand to other platforms, it's best for you to do all the analysis you did for your social strategy on Facebook before you move into these other platforms for social giving.

Instagram

Instagram is a photo- and video-sharing app that first launched in 2010. With one million users signing up within two months and over ten million in a year, Instagram's popularity skyrocketed quickly. In 2012, Facebook purchased the app for $1.0 billion, the most expensive tech acquisition to date. At the time, many considered this hefty sum to be a huge mistake on Mark Zuckerberg's part. Since then, Instagram has proven to be a valuable asset in Meta's portfolio.

As the platform has evolved, its simple esthetic and ease of use have made it popular with younger crowds. In 2022, social media users aged sixteen through twenty-five named Instagram as their favorite app.[26] As of right now, Instagram is the app where you can fundraise with a younger and more socially minded crowd.

Even though it was purchased by Meta, Instagram's social giving tools are slightly different from the ones you'd find on Facebook. Users are still able to run their own fundraising campaign whether that be for a marathon, a readathon, or even a pie eating contest. Nonprofits that want to be involved in these fundraisers must be verified through Facebook's Fundraising Page and also allow Meta Pay. Instagram's social fundraisers have three methods to post about fundraising: Posts, Stories, and Reels. Posts are displayed on a user's profile and within the feed of their followers. They may also show up on a user's "Explore" page, a page that highlights posts that align with a user's interests. If a post has a fundraiser attached, the link to donate will appear below the posted photo.

Instagram Stories are temporary posts that disappear after twenty-four hours. Reels are video content like Posts, but can also be used as Stories. Reels are Instagram's answer to TikTok. They're a way to create and discover short, entertaining videos on Instagram. Reels invite you to create fun videos to share with your friends or anyone on Instagram. You can record and edit fifteen-second multiclip videos with audio, effects, and other creative tools. For Stories and Reels, Instagram users have the option to add fundraising stickers. These allow their viewers to click through to a fundraising page and make their donation. While Instagram's giving tools are powered by Facebook, donor information isn't transferred so there is no way to track who is giving through Instagram and why.

---

26   Ibid.

It is also tougher to send messages (Direct Messages) to users on Instagram. This blocks any capacity for relationship building with donors and social fundraisers on Instagram. Essentially, it's a one-time transaction with no way to follow up or engage.

While Instagram's giving capabilities are still nascent, we believe that it's probably the next platform to become popular for social giving. Users are already creating their own fundraising campaigns and using those donations to support causes they believe in. Yet, the nonprofits that benefit from these fundraisers aren't able to connect with their donors due to Instagram's lack of community building tools like Facebook's groups. And with direct messaging only allowed by users who follow each other, nonprofits can't even start a conversation with their fundraisers on Instagram. They're unable to make deeper connections with their Instagram following that could generate more continual support. While many nonprofits operate Instagram accounts, they primarily use them for storytelling like broadening their messaging and sharing their impact. In the next few years, however, things may change. Instagram's current users are growing older and are becoming more interested in fundraising. To capitalize on that, Instagram continues to experiment with use cases that could make it the next hub of social giving.

LinkedIn

Since its creation in 2003, LinkedIn has helped professionals and businesses connect to fill open positions and network with other like-minded individuals. In the last few years, however, the platform has expanded to allow members to post about their perspectives on work and career advancement. Due to their positioning, many members exclusively use LinkedIn for building relationships with professional colleagues while they use Instagram and Facebook to stay connected with their friends and family as well as nonprofits and businesses they support. Unlike Meta's platforms, however, LinkedIn does not yet have a way to accept donations. That doesn't preclude LinkedIn users from social fundraising on their platform, however! Many savvy social fundraisers use the platform to direct back to larger social giving fundraisers hosted on other forms of social media like Facebook.

LinkedIn Ads are a great way to boost your Challenges on Facebook to audiences outside of your Facebook followers. By using the same methods that you did to create your original ads for your Challenge on Facebook, you can reach new audiences of coworkers and colleagues on LinkedIn. We've seen this with a few of the Challenges on Facebook we've coordinated, and it provides some boost to the overall fundraising. Additionally, LinkedIn has created a Nonprofit Hub that they advertise as helping nonprofits to "elevate their fundraising." These tools can be used to hire new talent, and there's some on attracting new donors through their messaging feature. That being said, we already know how pushing users off platform creates a snag in the social fundraising experience. For now, use LinkedIn to direct users back to your Facebook fundraising efforts.

YouTube

The original video platform that was one of the essential building blocks of the internet has gone through quite a few evolutions in its history. From the "Broadcast Yourself" era to live streaming to its purchase by and integration with Google, YouTube is still one of the most popular social media platforms. As a matter of fact, YouTube is the second most popular social media platform with 122 daily active users streaming billions of hours of content every day.[27]

Out of all of the social platforms we've mentioned in this chapter, YouTube's social giving tools are perhaps the most mature. Donors are able to give easily through a fundraise button that appears on

---

27   YouTube. https://blog.youtube/press/.

live streams and videos, though there is a caveat. In order to set up a YouTube Giving fundraiser, your channel—or personal profile—must have at least ten thousand subscribers. In the past few years, YouTube has largely been built around influencer content, channels with millions of followers that can guarantee ad revenue for the site. Users like game streamer PewDiePie and child content creators Cocomelon garner millions of views for the site and may drown out your message.

While your nonprofit's YouTube channel may have tons of followers, think carefully about how you want to use YouTube's giving tools to maximize your fundraising potential. Is your audience primed to watch a live stream from your nonprofit? How are you marketing this live stream? Are there influencers on YouTube that care about your cause that can help amplify your message? YouTube can be a crowded field—make sure your message stands out.

Twitch

Many social media platforms offer elements of live streaming nowadays. Whether you go live on Instagram for a makeup tutorial or live stream a cooking demonstration on Facebook, there's a huge market out there for people who want to watch other people do things. Twitch is one such platform that was built out of this desire to sit on the sidelines and watch. Built to allow users to livestream whatever game they were playing, Twitch has exploded into every medium with thirty-one million users each day.[28] In 2022, twitch.tv was one of the top twenty visited websites in the world.[29] Now, users can live stream anything they want within Twitch's guidelines—from the latest Call of Duty to making your mom's famous lasagna recipe. Within this community,

---

28   Twitch, https://www.twitch.tv/p/press-center/.

29   Kemp, "Digital 2022: Global overview report."

streamers are able to interact directly with those watching them play, creating deep connections and conversations.

Twitch offers a variety of tools from third parties to enable social giving on their live streams, and have even rolled out their own charity tools. One of the most popular of these tools is from a company known as Tiltify. Their focus is helping live streamers raise funds for causes and nonprofits they care about. Just like Twitch, Tiltify has learned how to gamify fundraising for live streamers everywhere. They provide tools that help streamers establish milestones, goals, and perks that incentivize those watching the stream to give. That being said, Tiltify—and other third-party integrations—direct users off platform to make their donation. And as it stands today, there's no function for a nonprofit to communicate with their donors through Twitch. Like many other platforms, there's a lot of promise here, but the use case is still not there.

There are a few examples of Twitch streamers making a real impact for social good, one of which was all thanks to one video game cat. In 2022, Annapurna Interactive, an American video game publisher, released *Stray*, a game where you play an adorable stray cat navigating a dystopian urban landscape full of alien creatures and robotic friends. The game struck a chord with gamers and cat-lovers alike—mainly because it was so gosh darn cute. Upon its release, Annapurna collaborated with the Nebraska Humane Society to host a Twitch livestream event where they raised over $7,000 for cats in their shelter. What's more, they reached a whole new donor base of gamers through their purr-fect campaign.

And this isn't the only example of Twitch streamers raising massive amounts for charity through streaming. Each year, Twitch Streamer DrLupo hosts his own charity stream for St. Jude Children's Research Hospital, which has raised over $3.68 million. In this digital-first event, he broadcasts directly into the homes of his over forty-four million followers to entertain and raise money for the fight against cancer. Fan bases build around these famous Twitch streamers, and we know what engaged digital communities can do when it comes to fundraising. It's thanks to these excited followers that Twitch raised over $83 million in 2020 alone.[30]

So, should your nonprofit get into Twitch streaming? Again, it depends. Just like YouTube, Twitch is largely dominated by influencers who have their own agenda and often require some form of payment. To get access to their devoted fan bases, you may have to engage these influencers, which can be tricky. Some nonprofits have found success in enlisting influencers to help their cause. No Kid Hungry, for example, has partnered with various food influencers, chefs, and restaurateurs to help raise funds for their cause. What's smart about these partnerships is that they enlisted aid from individuals whose personal and professional mission matches the nonprofit. This comes back to deeply knowing your mission, and who else calls that mission their own.

Facebook—For Now

As other social media platforms begin to create social giving tools, Facebook dominates when it comes to cultivating and supporting a sustainable donor base through social giving. The native use cases for these other platforms are just not there yet. While giving tools might be available on the platform, many of them direct donors to other sites or applications to give. This extra step in the process hamstrings your fundraising capability and loses you valuable donor information.

---

30 Chris Strub, "$83M+ raised and counting in 2020: Are Twitch streamers the new philanthropists?" Forbes, December 18, 2020, https://www.forbes.com/sites/chrisstrub/2020/12/18/83m-raised-and-counting-in-2020-are-twitch-streamers-the-new-philanthropists.

Additionally, many of these platforms lack conversational messaging. The ability to reach out directly to your donors is essential in maintaining and creating relationships with each of them. Finally, the audience on Facebook is vast when you compare it to those who use these other platforms. Unless you are trying to target a specific population, sticking to Facebook is your best bet.

Despite all this, if you are still considering whether or not to use a platform for a social giving campaign, ask yourself the following questions:

- Are giving tools on this social platform enabled?

- Is conversational messaging possible on this platform?

- Are the potential donations and revenue coming from this platform meaningful enough to impact your nonprofit?

If the answer to at least two of these questions is yes, then it's worth a shot. But remember, having an established social giving strategy on Facebook will be invaluable as you expand into this new platform. In other words, don't get too ahead of yourself, or you risk wasting valuable time and resources on an unsure bet.

As for TikTok and its social giving journey, they have since rolled out a whole new suite of giving tools that match the way people use their app. Through advanced analytics and promoted hashtags, users are able to join Challenges—much like Facebook—to help out causes that matter to them. These Challenges spread awareness for specific causes that users care about. TikTok has also donated funds in kind based on these Challenges and amplified certain nonprofit's messages when appropriate. To date, however, there's still no function to donate through the app. But that may change soon.

In fact, many of the ways we use the internet are changing. Right now, in 2023, we're seeing the dawn of a new era of the internet. Terms like Web 3.0, blockchain, cryptocurrency, and metaverse cover tech blogs in every corner of the internet. The once-admired behemoths of tech like Facebook, Twitter, and Apple are all struggling to compete with new upstarts like TikTok. We are on the precipice of another sea change, and how these changes will impact social giving and philanthropy as a whole are still unknown. With a solid social giving strategy, however, there's no way you can get lost in the noise.

Nick's Tips

- Establish a strong social giving strategy based on Meta's social giving tools before expanding into other social platforms.

- Know what you're getting into with other social media platforms!

  □ Instagram's tools enable on-platform giving but do not allow for conversational messaging.

  □ LinkedIn has very little in the philanthropy space but their ad capability is useful in directing their users back to your Facebook Challenges.

  □ YouTube and Twitch's social giving tools are largely third party and center around live streaming. Consider this when hosting a livestream event for your nonprofit.

- Ultimately, when considering another platform for social giving, you must know three things: whether giving tools are enabled, whether conversational messaging is allowed on the platform, and if the fundraising potential from the platform is worth the investment.

CHAPTER EIGHT

Emerging Technologies and the Giving Experience

Last Christmas, I received an Oculus VR headset from my wife as a gift. We're not big gamers in the Berman household, but it was exciting to try out a new piece of technology that's been getting a lot of buzz. Meta, Facebook's parent company, has put a big bet on Virtual Reality (VR) technology. A $2 billion bet, in fact, as that's how much they spent to buy the Oculus company in 2014.[31] The headset simulates real-world experiences all without leaving the comfort of a three-foot radius around your body. To test it out, I downloaded a free poker game that promised a fully immersive casino experience. So, I strapped on the headset, booted up the game, and less than three

---

31 Oscar Gonzales, "Facebook drops oculus name as part of meta rebrand," CNET, October 28, 2021, https://www.cnet.com/tech/facebook-drops-oculus-name-as-part-of-meta-rebrand/.

inches from my eyes appeared a card table in a casino. Seated at the table are about three or four other computer-generated players. I take the empty seat. At the beginning, it was a pretty accurate representation of poker—placing your bets, folding, calling. All the good stuff.

But then I started to overhear the conversations of the other players. With coughs, and ums, and natural cadences, the voices didn't sound anything like the computer-generated players with whom I thought I was playing. So, I said into my headset's microphone: "Are you guys real?" Turns out, they were! Other players from around the world who had downloaded the exact same software as I did were now playing poker with me. It was almost like I was in a real casino without any of the noise or cigar smoke. The headset made it so that it felt like we were all in the same room together—not thousands of miles away in a room wearing a silly headpiece. This virtual technology has the potential to change the way we use the internet and to make us feel closer to each other through a digital space.

While VR technology isn't new (it was first developed and used by an Air Force engineer back in 1966), it has taken many years and iterations to make it viable in the commercial market today. In 2023, there are many emerging technologies that stand to shape the way we, and future generations, engage with each other, with brands, and with nonprofit organizations. As a nonprofit leader, understanding how these innovations can be integrated into your fundraising campaign will give you a leg up on more antiquated organizations. While there are countless innovations happening every day that may change the fundraising landscape, I want to highlight two emerging technologies that can impact your nonprofit: virtual and augmented reality, and cryptocurrency.

Virtual and Augmented Reality—Demonstrating Impact with Immediacy

As mentioned earlier, virtual and augmented reality have the potential to bring a sense of togetherness to the digital space that's never been possible before. Through the Oculus and other VR technologies, people are able to connect more easily with each other while playing games or spending time together in the virtual world. For example, a friend of mine once told me about buying an Oculus for his dad, who lived across the country from him. He thought it would be a good way to stay in touch, and even downloaded a mini-golf game onto the device so they could relive memories of hitting the putting green in real life. What they found, however, was that very little of their time was spent making putts. Instead, they used the virtual green as a place to chat for hours.

It's stories like these that Mark Zuckerberg and the folks at Meta are trying to build the metaverse around. These moments of connection in a fully immersive world allow for users to connect with each other, no matter where they are. This potential connectivity, however, isn't reserved only for family and friends. Virtual and augmented reality can also be used to connect people to a nonprofit's mission and demonstrate the impact of their work.

One example of this is St. Jude Children's Research Hospital and their collaboration with Meta's "VR for Good Campaign." In order to demonstrate the impact of their donor's contributions, they designed a VR Experience called *Hall of Heroes* where donors can browse a virtual hall of statues of childhood cancer survivors and hear their stories. Through this technology, St. Jude's team offers a new take on the old and tired impact pamphlet and, instead, immerses their donors fully into their mission and its impact.

Augmented reality (AR) is a slightly different—and perhaps more accessible—take on creating new realities on top of our existing one. AR uses a smartphone's camera and adds additional images or badges to whatever you're capturing. To best understand AR, look to the first successful implementation of this technology: Pokémon GO. In July 2016, this augmented reality mobile game, developed by Niantic, Inc., had the whole world tied to their phones as users ran around their neighborhood trying to catch a Pikachu or Eevee to add to their collection of Pocket Monsters. To catch the Pokémon, you'd have to point your camera where the app directed you, and the monster would appear on your phone screen for you to catch. While it had some bugs, the game was so popular that it had been downloaded over 500 million times by the end of the year and paved the way for new innovations in AR technology.

While AR has proven to be useful for large companies, and marketing campaigns, there still hasn't been a good use case for non-profits using it to raise funds or increase donor engagement. That being said, imagine the possibilities for an organization like the World Wildlife Fund. With a simple QR code on branded material, they could project polar bears in their natural habitat to highlight the importance of saving these majestic creatures. Or the American Red Cross could use AR technology to direct users to the closest location to donate blood. With any tactic you use to engage your donor base, remember the vital rule we've discussed throughout the book—always connect it back to your mission.

VR and AR technologies are other tools for you to tell your nonprofit's story and how you are effecting change. Through these emerging technologies, nonprofits are able to simulate that in-person experience that inspires so many to give, and at a fraction of the cost. A shelter can host a virtual "Meet the Pets" event where they can match pets up for adoption with new forever homes. A cancer research institute could put donors right in the lab with scientists who are working on a cure. The options are near limitless. But, even when designing these kinds of events, remember to stay authentic. Donors and your social fundraisers want to hear their impact, but never want to feel like they're being "sold to."

Cryptocurrency and Crypto Giving Populations

In 2023, cryptocurrency is a topic that is nearly ubiquitous. Everyone from your uncle at Christmas to the barista that makes your coffee to nightly news anchors seem to have a take about this new and digital currency. And yet, the concept of cryptocurrency is still elusive to many people. To define it in the most basic sense, cryptocurrency is a digital currency that is built off of blockchain technology and can be bought or sold using a cryptowallet. Blockchain technology provides a decentralized, secure, and transparent system for recording and validating cryptocurrency transactions. As a decentralized currency, cryptocurrency eliminates the need for a central authority like a government and instead distributes the power and control to the network participants. To secure crypto transactions, blockchain technology creates a unique hash that links each transaction to the previous one. This, as well as a publicly visible ledger of transactions, makes it nearly impossible to alter transaction data without detection. As this ledger grows with each transaction, it becomes incredibly difficult to modify. Combined with powerful consensus algorithms, these mechanisms enable the network to reach agreement on the transaction data without the need for a central authority. These algorithms make it so cryptocurrency can serve both as a currency and a publicly available accounting system. Bitcoin, ethereum, and even the memeable Dogecoin are all examples of different cryptocurrencies that users can treat like any other currency, without being based in any one central bank or government.

Sounds complicated? That's because crypto can be, but it's also lucrative. In 2021, when crypto first began to gain popularity, a lot of people made a lot of money. With this surge in wealth, people who have never considered donating to charity now have the potential to do so through their cryptowallets. Just like social giving and Meta's nonprofit tools expanded philanthropy into new donor populations, cryptocurrency is also creating new populations of donors. New crypto-minded audiences may present an opportunity for nonprofits to increase their fundraising efforts. Additionally, because crypto fluctuates based on its user base, donations made in cryptocurrency have the potential to appreciate in value over time. And, with its blockchain ledger system, these donations are more secure and allow for anonymous donations to be made.

Yet, receiving donations through cryptocurrency is not as easy as getting a check or a direct deposit. It can be a confusing process that requires new tax reporting methods and signing up for your own cryptowallet. Some organizations, like Engiven and BitGive, work with nonprofits to enable donations in crypto. These groups manage your crypto donations, and either maintain them in their original cryptocurrency or transfer them to fiat—what cryptonerds call traditional forms of currency. Nonprofits like The Salvation Army and No Kid Hungry have begun to accept cryptocurrency as donations to test out how crypto can impact their fundraising potential. To reduce the friction in the giving process, consider investing in your own cryptowallet. There are many young folks who have a lot of net worth in cryptocurrency. Turning on crypto donations for your nonprofit will make it easier for them to contribute to your cause.

These new technologies are exciting, no doubt about it. To the nonprofit, they offer up new ways to connect with their audiences and reduce friction for potential unrealized donors. Despite all this, however, these technologies are outside the reach of many nonprofits. The biggest gain for your nonprofit today is to continue to invest in creating frictionless giving experience empowered by the compelling story of your organization and its impact on your cause. As giving trends change and technologies evolve, remember these, and you'll know exactly where to invest your time. Doing so will ensure that you engage an excited audience of donors who see themselves as part of your organization.

Nick's Tips

- Stay up-to-date on emerging technology trends to understand how they will impact your nonprofit's fundraising efforts.

- Using virtual and augmented reality technologies can highlight your nonprofit's impact in an immediate way. It also connects your donors to your mission in ways that traditional marketing does not.

- Investing in cryptocurrency will reduce friction for key donors who wish to contribute to your cause.

CHAPTER NINE

Artificial Intelligence and the *Next* Next Wave for Nonprofits

Let me tell you how I've been putting together my grocery list lately. (I swear it's related to nonprofit work!) A couple of months ago, my wife decided to try and include more vegetables in our meals throughout the week. As part of that, she's adopted a vegetarian diet. The one difficulty is protein—we're a pretty active family that needs to refuel. While browsing recipe sites, she complained to me that it was difficult to find high-protein vegetarian recipes without eating tofu every single day. It sounded like she needed a meal plan, but she didn't have time to do her own research. And with our schedule and budgeting, sourcing and hiring a nutritionist was just out of the question. As soon as I heard her request, however, I knew that ChatGPT, a tool I had been tinkering with at work, could help.

Developed by OpenAI, ChatGPT was one of the first artificial intelligence (AI) algorithms to be made available to the public. Its technology empowers users to input complex queries that it can answer in the matter of seconds. The AI takes the prompt and scans the internet to help it build an accurate response and delivers it all to the user in an easily digestible format. It's able to respond to intricate questions, provide advice, do data analysis, and so much more. Since its launch in 2023, it has dominated the media with stories about its shocking capabilities. ChatGPT has broken open the world of AI, creating huge opportunities for how we use technology. Every one of the big players, from Microsoft to Google to Amazon, are rolling out their own versions of AI to compete. And just like everyone else, I have been fascinated with it and test out its capabilities at every opportunity.

So when my wife told me what she was looking for in a meal plan it sounded like the perfect ChatGPT prompt. I pulled up the platform and typed in the following query:

Provide me with a meal plan for five days, three meals each day, that is vegetarian and high in protein. Each recipe will only include five ingredients with alternative protein options to tofu.

After a few moments, the text box began to populate with recipes for a five-day meal plan that were vegetarian but didn't overwhelm the eater with tofu. What is wild is that the protein sources were also listed, so I could easily see the macros. They even provided ingredients and suggestions of brands to purchase. To further simplify my life, I took it a step further with this next prompt:

Give me a grocery list based on the menu provided.

From there, ChatGPT gave me an itemized list that I could easily drop into my Instacart account for next-day delivery.

What would have taken me an hour of Google searches with cross-referencing recipe websites, and nutrition pages, only took ChatGPT thirty seconds. (I shudder at how long it would have taken if you only had a library as your source for research.) Now, the algorithm is still learning so some of the recipes needed a little editing from my part. That being said, it automated a task that I might not have had the time to take on myself. With very little effort on my part, ChatGPT was able to fully answer a complex question with a solution that was 95 percent of the way there. All I needed to worry about was actually cooking the meal—something AI can't do with my kitchen...yet.

My experience with ChatGPT illustrates only a fraction of the possibilities presented by AI. This emerging technology stands to change nearly everything. On par with inventions like the internet and mobile phone technology, every industry including the nonprofit sector will be changed thanks to AI. While machine learning technology has been in development for the past twenty years, its most recent advances have made it so that AI's capabilities will soon be commonplace in many industries. Those who do not adapt will be left behind. Even as far back as 2018, the *Harvard Business Review* was writing articles with the headline "Why Companies That Wait to Adopt AI May Never Catch Up," and that was before ChatGPT was even a twinkle in Sam Altman's eye.[32]

---

32 Vikram Mahidar and Thomas Davenport, "Why companies that wait to adopt AI may never catch up," Harvard Business Review, December 6, 2018, https://hbr.org/2018/12/why-companies-that-wait-to-adopt-ai-may-never-catch-up#:~:text=By%20the%20time%20a%20late,adopters%20may%20never%20catch%20up.

Nonprofits who seek to make an impact cannot afford to wait to adopt AI technology. While you know how social giving has revolutionized fundraising from the topics in this book, you should also know that the next big wave of change is already here, and it's AI. Through the capabilities and tools made possible through AI, nonprofits can reach out to their community, better understand their data, and tell their organization's stories of impact. And it's not happening tomorrow, these capabilities are here today. In less than three years, using AI tools will become standard for nonprofits, and the organizations that choose to ignore its potential will only be making space for other more sophisticated nonprofits. The new capabilities present in AI make it so your nonprofit can do more with less, allowing you to focus on your organization's cause.

How Nonprofits Can Use AI Today

At an investor dinner I attended, there was a speaker who gave a presentation on the potential of AI and its implications on the nonprofit industry. In his speech, he described the development and adoption of this new technology with a fable about the inventor of chess. The story goes that when chess was first invented, the king of a great country wanted it so much that he offered the game's creator anything he wanted in the kingdom. The inventor thought for a moment and then made his offer. The price for chess was as such: place one grain of rice on the first square of the chess board. Then on the two squares that touch it, place two grains. With every square, the amount of rice would double, and the number of squares would grow. Thinking this was a steal, the king agreed. It wasn't until his men began counting the grains of rice they would need that they realized there was not enough rice in the kingdom.

This chess board analogy has often been used to describe the exponential growth of computer technology of the past twenty years. Many have said that we are on the "back half of the chessboard" when it comes to the exponential growth of computer technologies. That the technological breakthroughs with our current technologies are growing fewer and fewer. For AI, however, we are still on the first half of the board. We still do not know all the ways in which AI will become embedded into our everyday lives. Each and every day new ground is being uncovered in the race to implement AI. With this new ground comes new possibilities for those who take advantage of these tools. While you may stand in awe of this new frontier of possibility, there are ways your nonprofit can use AI even today to power up your operations.

One of those ways your nonprofit can harness AI's power will help you demonstrate the impact of your work at scale. Every day at GoodUnited, we receive thousands and thousands of success stories from nonprofits thanks to Messenger-enabled one-to-one chats. All of this data are unstructured. It takes our team a long time to read through these stories, categorize them, understand the salient information, and pull impact statements. ChatGPT helps us see what's underneath all of that data. By feeding these stories of impact into its algorithm, it can provide us with a very basic sentiment analysis, and even pick out case studies and anecdotes. We then take this information and apply it to our other activities, be they challenge content or direct messaging to donors and fundraisers. This analytical work of trudging through a mess of data would have taken our team a couple of days just to get through. And in another week, they may have an analysis deck with suggested action items. With ChatGPT's general solution, we can focus on implementing those ideas rather than the busywork of analyzing.

Being able to detect trends is one of ChatGPT's super powers. With the whole internet's understanding of data science at its fingertips, it can show you the "so what?" of your data so you can take action. At GoodUnited, we used ChatGPT to help us better understand a specific Facebook Challenge we were running with one of our partners. This specific challenge had generated tons of data, everything from the donor's name to the amount donated to the motivating factors that inspired them to give. To hasten the analysis, we put that dataset into ChatGPT (ensuring that we scrubbed for personally identifiable information) to understand the trends and movements of our partner's Facebook Challenge. ChatGPT was able to summarize the results, describe the trends, and even point out the donors that were most likely to give again. The AI even gave me a Google Sheets formula that I could tinker with to do its analysis on my own.

In the near future, AI may also be able to help nonprofits through advanced predictive analytic tools that identify new potential donors. While we put a lot of effort into researching audiences and personas today, AI can do this work with less time and more accuracy than we ever could. By using AI to analyze data on donor behavior, nonprofits will be able to predict which donors are most likely to make a donation and to further segment their donors based on this likelihood. This helps nonprofits strategize their outreach efforts to target the specific audiences that are ready to give. It's clear that predictive analytics through AI saves nonprofits time and effort. With this work done, they're able to allocate their resources toward individuals that are primed to donate.

Finally, nonprofits can use ChatGPT for support on their marketing and strategy. If you're looking to build your nonprofit's social media following, consistency of voice and tone is key. By giving

ChatGPT just a little information about your nonprofit, it can create social media strategies, content calendars, posts, and even social fundraising ideas. Use this below prompt to generate a social media strategy from ChatGPT in a matter of seconds:

Use the information below to generate a creative social media content calendar for a nonprofit organization for the next week:

Nonprofit Name: [Enter your organization's name]

Nonprofit Website: [Your website]

Mission of nonprofit: [The mission statement of your nonprofit]

Goals for social media: [Detail what you want to accomplish with social media]

Attributes of social media followers: [Describe your donors and potential donors that you want to attract]

Channel: [Here put all the platforms that you will be using for social media]

For context, here's an example of this prompt from Nick's nonprofit, Stop Soldier Suicide:

Use the information below to generate a creative social media content calendar for a nonprofit for the next week:

Nonprofit Name: Stop Soldier Suicide

Nonprofit Website: www.stopsoldiersuicide.org

Mission of nonprofit:
- Reduce service member and veteran suicide using enhanced data insights, focused client acquisition, and suicide-specific intervention services.
- A nation where service members & veterans have no greater risk for suicide than any other American.

Goals for social media: Increase engagement and community

Demographic of social media followers:
- Veteran and active duty service members
- 60% women, 40% men

Channel:
- Facebook

But it's not just copy or strategy that AI can provide. With AI image generators from Bing or Midjourney, you can type in what image you need, and in moments you'll have an image you can use for a social media post or newsletter. Need a banner image of a marathon runner for your post encouraging people to sign up for your 5k? Just type in the prompt to Midjourney and you'll have something eye-catching without having to get a graphic design degree. In a world where marketing boils down to what catches people's attention, these kinds of images are essential in enticing potential donors.

As covered in previous chapters, ChatBots are already changing the way we interface with companies and institutions across industry. Both nonprofit and for-profit organizations use this AI to handle support requests, answer frequently asked questions, and navigate users to the right person to help them. We've also shown you how the nonprofits that we partner with at GoodUnited use AI to connect to their donor base through Facebook Messenger. Yet, these technologies are just barely scratching the surface of the full capabilities of AI. New AI technologies like ChatGPT will allow for more personalized communications, more precise analytics, and a targeted approach to fundraising through social media.

As you know, GoodUnited helps nonprofits stay in touch and build one-on-one relationships with their donor base by creating personal messaging tailored to the individual. As the technology stands today, Facebook users have to opt into their interests by "liking" something or by openly admitting their interests to the AI running the Messenger experience. With more advanced AI, this may no longer be necessary. In the (again, near) future, AI can be used to analyze data on donors' past interactions on social media and elsewhere on the internet to determine their preferences and passions. This will enable nonprofits to send highly personalized fundraising messages that are more likely to inspire real donations. With these emerging predictive analytics, nonprofits will be able to reach the right person with the right message at the right time with pinpoint accuracy.

It's clear that AI-based tools will be instrumental in almost every industry in the near future, and tech-averse nonprofits must adopt or they will lose it all. AI will help craft effective social giving campaigns for nonprofits. With audience segmentation analytics and donor behavior data, AI ensures that your campaigns resonate with your specific targeted audiences. And on top of all that, AI can write challenge messaging, engaging Facebook Ads, and unique Messenger copy to encourage and motivate your social fundraisers. AI does every-thing that takes us hours to do in a fraction of that time. It's raising the floor of what's possible for your organization, saving your people the time to do what you hired them to do—make a difference.

Many AI naysayers, however, have emerged from the deepest corners of the internet bemoaning how this new technology will cost us our jobs. These machines will take over our businesses and organizations, and the humans won't be able to take it back. To me, this reads more like a plot from a *Terminator* movie than the reality of AI. It's true that AI will be able to take on a lot of the tasks once performed by your data analytics or creative team, but that doesn't mean these employees become obsolete. In an organization that uses AI, employees focus on the human tasks that require action, rather than spending time analyzing or brainstorming. And even the most advanced AI makes miscalculations. When that time comes, it's experienced humans who will need to make the adjustments. AI is a tool, not a replacement for the talent of your employees.

And if we treat it like a tool, there's no limit to what we can do with it. Nonprofits that are historically tech-averse must adopt AI technology or face falling into obscurity. It is imperative that your nonprofit becomes more familiar with how AI can serve your organization, today, so that you can be prepared for how AI will affect your tomorrow. The longer you take, the less you'll be able to do. This technology stands to change the way we all interact with the world. If you are not prepared, the great work you're doing will all be for naught, and your donor base will quickly shift to a nonprofit that's powered by AI.

Nick's Tips

- Take advantage of the possibilities AI has made possible today to prepare your organization for the future of AI.

- Use ChatGPT to create social media strategies and social calendars that reach the donors you need today.

- Feed raw data from your nonprofit into ChatGPT to gain insights into the movements of your donor base that can inform future social giving campaigns.

- Develop new images for marketing and social with Midjourney or Bing to grab the attention of potential donors.

One-Click to Grow

Jeremy: Fundraising is a tough business. Through our partnerships with our clients, we've seen firsthand the hard work that they put into raising the funds they need to accomplish their missions.

Nick: So many of our clients spend a huge amount of their time fundraising. It can become all-consuming and distracting from your organization's mission. Truly, it can feel like you're making no progress, especially when your fundraising is locked into tactics like newsletters, e-blasts, and gala events.

Jeremy: That's not to say that those tactics aren't valuable, but they can miss the mark if you aren't listening to your donors and fundraisers. But there's another way possible. Through social giving, you will be able to establish a one-on-one relationship with all of your donors and supercharge their giving potential. But if you've gotten this far, you know that already.

The days of direct mailers are fading. Today's generation of donors are giving more and more through social media, the digital space where they spend a majority of their time. To futureproof your nonprofit, develop a social giving strategy that includes all members of your organization—from the "gives-five-dollar-a-month" contributor all the way up to your legacy donors. To keep them coming back, you have to understand their support for your cause and how they see themselves in your organization. And you have to know their stories so that you can establish authentic connections with those who support your cause. Social giving tools give you the capability to do this at scale and allow you to create these meaningful relationships with your base.

Nick: In my experience leading a nonprofit with a social giving strategy, I appreciate how conversational messaging gives me a direct insight into the lives of my donors. Through Facebook messaging, I understand what my donors are going through and why they choose to give. I also know their interests so that our relationship can be more than just a transaction. I know, for example, that "Julie" donates for her son, a serviceman returning from active duty who struggles with his transition back. I also know that Julie's family loves the Phillies, and they go to Veteran Night at the Citizen Bank Park whenever they can. This insight allows me to plan digital and in-person events that appeal to people like Julie and her family.

Jeremy: And with digital events like Facebook Challenges, we're able to blow up the reach of previously in-person events. And the momentum just keeps growing. Social fundraisers who believe in the mission of a nonprofit raise funds for their birthdays or special occasions. Challenges encourage this throughout the year and create a community around the energy of these ardent supporters. And the connections made through these Facebook Challenge groups provide a sense of community for your nonprofit and cultivate lifelong support for your cause. The momentum keeps building.

There's a lot more on the horizon for the world of giving. And just like with the advent of social giving, things are bound to change. By adopting the lessons in this book about social giving, however, you prepare your nonprofit for the *next* next wave. We're already seeing how innovations in AI impact the nonprofit world. But what will come after that? And how are you preparing?

Nick: With their almost translucent margins, it is easy to see why nonprofits can be risk-averse when it comes to new technology. I understand that firsthand. For those who still have questions about social giving, this technology no longer represents a risky move to me as a nonprofit leader. As a matter of fact, it has never been easier for someone to make a donation to Stop Soldier Suicide. Frictionless one-click to give methods make the giving process incredibly simple. It's clear that social giving is the way forward for philanthropy. If you still have misgivings, reach out to me, and I can tell you personally how these tools have changed the game for my nonprofit.

Jeremy: Again, traditional fundraising is hard. But people love to give, especially when they feel a personal connection to a mission. Through social giving, you can give them that and so much more. So why make it any more difficult than it already is? Give your donors that one-click experience they crave and see how much more your nonprofit can do—empowered by social giving.

ABOUT THE AUTHORS

Jeremy Berman is the president and CEO of GoodUnited. His mission is to democratize the nonprofit supporter experience by empowering nonprofits to build a relationship with every supporter. He has also served as the director of StartUp Grind where he worked to build a passionate startup community in Charleston, South Carolina. He holds an MBA from the University of North Carolina's Kegan-Flagler Business School.

Nick Black is the cofounder and CEO of GoodUnited. He is also the cofounder and vice chairman of the Board for Stop Soldier Suicide, the first national civilian nonprofit dedicated to preventing active duty and veteran suicide. He also holds an MBA from the University of North Carolina's Kegan-Flagler Business School.

They both reside in Charleston, South Carolina.